The Zebra Cookbook

Have fun making your own cakes and tasty snacks and then go on to prepare meals for your friends and family.

The instructions in this cookbook are so easy to follow that you will be able to learn to cook all by yourself.

Cover illustration by Desmond Clover.

The Zebra Cookbook

Maureen Williams

Evans Brothers Limited London

Published by Evans Brothers Limited
Montague House, Russell Square,
London, W.C.1

First published 1971
Third printing 1974

Set in 11 on 12 pt Baskerville
Printed in Great Britain
by Cox & Wyman Ltd.,
London, Reading and Fakenham.

CSD ISBN 0 237 35198 6
PB   ISBN 0 237 35202 8

PRA 3552

Contents

	Gas Numbers	Celsius	Fahrenheit
Cool or Slow	R1	90°C	200°F
	R$\frac{1}{2}$	105°C	225°F
	R1	120°C	250°F
	R2	135°C	275°F
Moderately Hot	R3	150°C	300°F
	R4	160°C	325°F
	R5	175°C	350°F
Hot	R6	190°C	375°F
	R7	205°C	400°F
Very Hot	R8	220°C	425°F
	R9	235°C	450°F
	R10	250°C	475°F
			500°F

The oven temperatures are written in the three different ways in the recipes. For example, you will find it written like this, R3/160°C/325°F which means that if you are cooking with gas you must set it at Regulo 3, but if you are cooking with electricity set it at 160°C or 325°F according to the way in which your cooker is marked.

Let's Look in the Kitchen

This section of the book is to introduce you to the kitchen and to let you practise using the big and small equipment that you find there. When you understand how to use the pieces of equipment, for example the cooker or the egg-whisk, then you can begin to prepare and cook food.

Sometimes you will have good results and sometimes they will not be so good at first. Remember that even the most experienced cooks have their off-days when things go wrong. If this is the case, you, like the best cooks, can ask yourself why it went wrong and in that way it need not happen again.

One important thing to remember, always taste your own cooking as you prepare it and just before you serve it. This, of course, is one of the most enjoyable parts of cooking! Keep a teaspoon in a basin of cold water on your work-top and each time you use your tasting spoon wash it and put it back in the cold water.

Measuring and Weighing

In cooking you will be following a recipe and a method in order to make something nice to eat. A recipe is a list of foodstuffs or ingredients and written beside each is the amount you need. A method is a list of instructions to help you make the dish. To be able to get the correct amount of foodstuffs or ingredients you must either count out, measure out, or weigh out accurately.

Counting out
This is the easiest method, but unfortunately it cannot be given for everything.

You will meet it like this:

4 rashers of bacon
2 eggs
4 slices of thick bread

Measuring out

Where it is not possible to give a number to count, the recipe gives a handy measurement. You will meet it like this:

1 teacup of milk
1 heaped tablespoon of flour
1 rounded tablespoon of sugar

Weighing out

If you have scales in your kitchen, then use them by all means. You just need to look at the bottom of each page where a recipe is given to find the ingredients in ounces or grammes to suit scales marked off in either Imperial or Metric units. You will meet:

Imperial measures like this:	Metric measures like this:
4 oz flour	115g flour
2 oz margarine	55g margarine
1 oz sugar	30g sugar

You have probably noticed already that some of the words given like tablespoon, ounce, gramme, etc., have a shortened version. The following list shows the shortened terms used in this book.

tablespoon = tbsp	teaspoon = tsp
ounce = oz	gramme = g
Fahrenheit = F	Celsius = C
degree = °	pint = pt
litre = l	centimetre = cm
inch = in	pound = lb
kilogram = kg	millilitres = ml

To get the right amount of any fat without weighing scales, you just start with a new block. This will either be a packet of 8 oz (½ lb) which is the Imperial measurement. Or it will be a packet of 250g (¼ kg) which is the Metric measurement. If you have an 8 oz packet of lard, margarine or butter, divide with a knife into 8 equal portions. Each equal portion should measure 1 oz.

1oz	1oz	1oz	1oz
1oz	1oz	1oz	1oz

8oz

25g	25g	25g	25g	25g
25g	25g	25g	25g	25g

250g

If you have a 250g packet of lard, margarine or butter, divide with a knife into 10 equal portions. Each equal portion should measure 25g.

In our recipes the handy measurements will give all fats in either '1 equal portion' or '2 equal portions' or '3 equal portions' and so on. Remember to read the amount on a new block of fat and divide it correctly.

To help you use handy measures accurately, follow these diagrams:

A heaped spoon.

A rounded spoon. As much above the spoon as in the bowl of the spoon.

A level spoon. Use a knife to level off the ingredients with the sides of the spoon.

Half a level spoon.

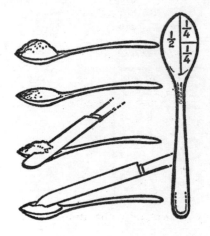

You will need this equipment

vegetable knife

cook's knife

vegetable peeler

bread knife

palette knife

fish slice

wooden spoon

whisk

colander

sieve

grater

dredger

mixing bowl

basin

measuring jug

sandwich tin

bun tin

baking tray

cooling tray

lemon squeezer

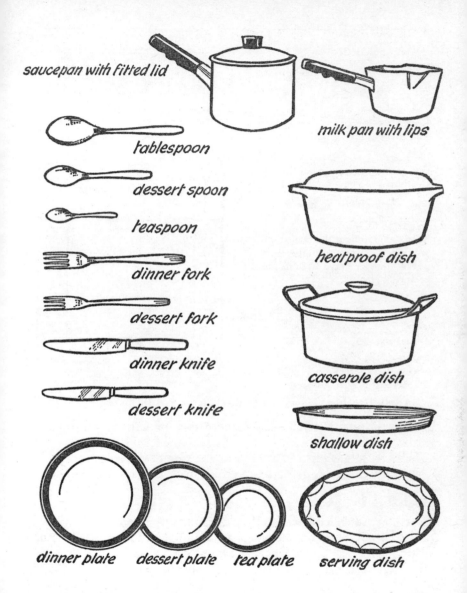

saucepan with fitted lid

milk pan with lips

tablespoon

dessert spoon

teaspoon

dinner fork

dessert fork

dinner knife

dessert knife

heatproof dish

casserole dish

shallow dish

dinner plate   dessert plate   tea plate   serving dish

The Cooker

Look at your cooker. You will find there are three main parts:

the rings
the grill
the oven

There may also be a place to warm the plates.

To be able to light the cooker you must first know whether it is gas or electric. The cooker in the picture is electric.

Lighting a gas cooker

You will be able to light each part in one of three ways:

1 Automatically, because there is a pilot light continually burning
2 By a 'gas pistol' hanging at the side of the cooker
3 By a match, or better because it is safer, by a taper

Lighting the gas rings

These are so called because they are made up of a ring of gas jets. If you are lighting the gas rings automatically, first pick the knob which sends gas to the ring you want to heat, turn the knob anti-clockwise and the gas flame should pop up.

If you are lighting the gas rings with a 'gas pistol' or a taper, turn the knob anti-clockwise and put the lighted gun or taper to the gas ring. Always hold a lighted 'gas pistol', match or taper UPRIGHT so that the flame burns away from your fingers. Only when you have turned the gas knob ON should you tilt the flame to the gas jets.

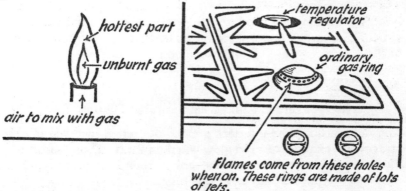

hottest part

unburnt gas

air to mix with gas

temperature regulator

ordinary gas ring

Flames come from these holes when on. These rings are made of lots of jets.

The gas oven

The first thing you must do every time you light a gas oven is OPEN THE OVEN DOOR. Now find the oven knob and you will see it is marked from ¼–9. These numbers on a gas cooker are known as Regulo ¼–9 or just R¼–9. Look on page 6 to find out more about the temperature of these Regulo markings. Now look for the gas jets in the oven. Are they at the sides or the back?

Because the oven is heated by convection or air currents, the top shelf of the oven is the hottest part, the middle shelf 10°F/4·5°C below the set temperature and the lowest 20°F/9°C cooler than the middle shelf.

The grill

The position of the grill may be anywhere between waist and eye level. It is made up of one or two long, straight gas jets.

Light the grill in the same way as you lit the gas ring.

Temperature (Thermo) Regulator

Fitted to the hot plate or ring of gas and electric cookers may be a Temperature (Thermo) Regulator. Follow the instruction booklet that was sent with the stove to find out the right number at which to set it for the food you are cooking.

Turning on an electric cooker

Near the cooker but fixed to the wall there should be a large switch. This switch must be ON for the electricity to be able to flow to the cooker. On top of your stove you may find

1. a radiant hot plate
2. a solid hot plate
3. a hot plate fitted with a Temperature (Thermo) Regulator.

The radiant hot plate is a dark grey colour when switched OFF or on LOW but changes to a red glow when on HIGH. If you look at the illustration you will see a tube going round in a spiral. The elements are packed tightly in this tube.

The solid hot plate is also dark grey in colour, but this does not change colour anytime when switched ON even when on HIGH.

Turning on the electric oven

To turn on the oven, you must make sure the switch on the wall is ON. Then find the oven knob and set it at the temperature you want your oven to reach. You will see it marked from 200° Fahrenheit to 500° Fahrenheit or 200°F to 500°F. Or you may have one marked from 100° Celsius to 250° Celsius or 100°C to 250°C. Be sure to find out whether the oven temperatures are marked in Fahrenheit or Celsius before you start cooking. Most cookers have a little bulb near the oven knob which lights up when the oven is switched on. This light will only go out when the oven heat has reached the temperature you set. The electric elements that heat the oven are usually placed each side and bulge out behind the metal lining of the oven. Sometimes they are at the top or bottom as well.

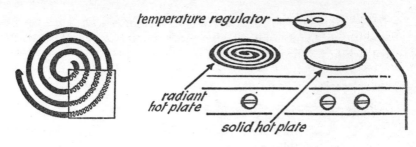

temperature regulator

radiant hot plate

solid hot plate

1.

2.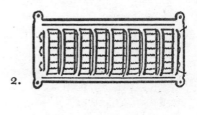

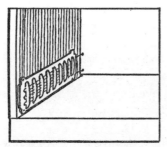

3.

Elements are made of thin wire (1) and are packed in hard cement (2) and fitted behind the oven lining (3).

Where there are side elements only, the top shelf of the oven is the hottest part with just a few degrees cooler in the middle and a few degrees cooler still at the bottom. If there is a bottom element as well as the two side ones, the bottom is as hot as the top. The middle shelf is the coolest part. The oven may take 10–14 mins. to heat up.

The electric grill

The position of the grill may be anywhere between waist and eye level. The grill, like the rings and the oven, is heated by elements.

Keeping plates warm on gas and electric cookers

If you are going to serve food hot, then the plates and dishes on which it is served should be warmed through beforehand. The hot food being dished on to a warm plate or dish will not lose heat so quickly as it would if dished on to cold containers. On most stoves you will be able to find somewhere safe to put plates and dishes to warm while you are cooking.

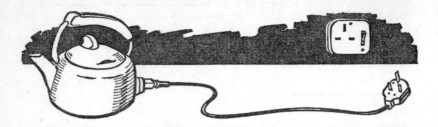

The electric kettle

Just as the ring on top of the stove, the oven and the grill all have elements which heat from a flow of electricity, you will also be able to see the element inside your kettle. An important part is the flex with a pin-point plug on one end that fits into the wall, and a plug on the other end that fits into the back of the kettle.

To fill with water, take just the kettle to the tap. Pour enough water in to make sure the element is completely covered otherwise it will be damaged during the time it is heating.

Fit the lid on, placing the steam vents or holes to the side of the handle. This way, when the kettle boils and steam gushes out of those vents your hand will not be scalded when you pick up the kettle. Carry back the kettle and stand it near to the wall socket.

1 Make sure you have perfectly DRY HANDS, if not, dry them now.
2 First push the kettle plug into the kettle socket.
3 Now before you touch the wall socket, make sure the switch on the wall is in the OFF position, if not, switch it OFF.
4 Push the pin point plug into the wall socket.
5 The last thing to do is to put the switch ON. When the kettle boils, the first thing to do is to put the switch OFF. Then pull out the socket from the kettle and use the water.

Cooking with care on top of the stove

1 Use a saucepan that covers the gas ring or electric hot-plate completely. Then you are making use of all the heat possible. Gas flames must always be underneath the saucepan. If they lick up the sides, then turn down the heat.

2 Beginner cooks will find a thick saucepan easier to use than a thin one as the contents will not burn so quickly.
It is essential that saucepans with flat, machined bases be used on solid hot plates and they are also best on radiant hot-plates. The flat, machined pans are made for electric stoves to pass all the heat from the element to the food evenly.

3 Always make sure that saucepan handles are in a safe place on the stove to avoid them getting knocked over or hot from another ring.

Cooking with care in the oven

1 All dishes should be put on baking trays to go into the oven as it will be easier for lifting out with TWO HANDS, but make sure there is 1 in or 2·5 cm space between the baking tray and the sides of the oven which are heated. Remember that if you cram one shelf with too much then the air currents will not be able to circulate properly. For the same reason always use the shelves of the oven, never the floor. There is usually a long side to a baking tray and a short side, put the long side of the baking tray parallel to the heat in the oven.

2 The hottest part of all ovens is the top shelf, so if you are cooking more than one item, make sure the item needing the highest temperature goes on the top shelf.

3 In cooking you are using hot things so you have to think carefully of what you are going to do next. Always know where you are going to put hot dishes which are taken from the oven. You can either stand them on a cool part of the stove or else on a heat-proof mat on your work-top. You could mark a plastic or wooden surface with a hot pan or dish. Always use an oven-cloth or oven gloves to move hot dishes, otherwise you may get a burn.

Let's Make Beefburger Rolls and Hot Chocolate

For 2

Food to collect	**Equipment to collect**

Food to collect

2 beefburgers
2 soft rolls
1 tin of drinking chocolate
2 teacupsful of milk

Equipment to collect

1 baking tray
1 milk saucepan
1 breadboard
1 kettle
1 teaspoon
1 knife and fork to turn over beefburgers
1 knife to cut rolls

Preparation

* Wash your hands. Put on your apron.
* Collect the food and equipment. Put neatly on the work-top.
* Put the oven on at R1/150°C/300°F. Put a shelf at the top of the oven. Make sure there is an oven-cloth nearby.
* Set the table as shown. Put the plates to warm and stand the mugs near the kettle.

For the table

2 place-mats or a cloth
2 paper serviettes
2 teaspoons
a sugar bowl and spoon
2 table-mats

PUT TO WARM
2 teaplates

PUT NEAR THE KETTLE
2 mugs

Method of work

1 Remembering everything about turning on or lighting a stove (see page 12), put the grill on HIGH or the highest number marked.

2 Place the beefburgers on the grid and put them under the grill.

3 Look at the time. Have you checked with the instructions on the packet for cooking time? Work out the time they will be ready.

4 Cut each roll through the middle. Put the top back on the bottom and stand both on the baking tray.

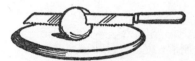 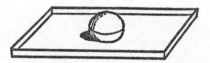

5 Put the rolls in the oven to warm through.

6 Fill the kettle with water and put it on to boil.

7 Into each mug put 1 teaspoon of drinking chocolate.

8 When the beefburgers are a deep brown on the first side, check with the time to see if they should be turned over. If so, use a knife and fork to turn them.

9 Measure out 2 teacupsful of milk and put it in a saucepan.

10 Take the pan to the stove, light a ring or turn on a hot-plate for the milk and set the knob at MEDIUM heat.

11 Now stand by the stove and keep a watchful eye on:

       * the beefburgers   (they could burn!)
       * the rolls   (they could become dry)
       * the kettle   (make sure it is really boiling)

When you first put the kettle on, the water is cold and fairly still. As it gets hotter the water begins to move and tiny bubbles start appearing at the sides. This is called SIMMERING point. At this stage a little steam is given off so do not think it is boiling. When the water begins moving about rapidly and large bubbles dance all over the top of the water, then the steam really gushes out of the spout and vent. This is called BOILING. If the kettle boils before you are ready to use it, just take it off the heat or turn it off until you need to use it. Then you must reboil it.

* the milk   (it could suddenly boil over)

Milk is also very still when it is cold. As it reaches SIMMERING point you will see tiny bubbles appearing at the sides of the pan. From this point onwards you must keep a very careful watch on the milk because as it comes to the boil it will suddenly rise in the pan and overflow on to the stove.
Aim to take the milk off the heat when you see TINY bubbles coming to the surface. As the bubbles become large you know that the milk is near to boiling up the sides of the pan.

12 As each item is ready, first turn off its source of heat.
13 If the milk is ready first, turn off the heat, pour into the mugs stirring as you pour. Then fill the saucepan with cold water and stand on a cool part of the stove or on a heat-proof mat.
14 When the kettle boils turn it off, top the mugs up with water and stir.
15 When the beefburgers are a deep brown on each side, turn off the grill and oven. On to the work-top put out the 2 warm plates, the 2 rolls and the 2 beefburgers.
16 Put one beefburger between each roll. Place one on each plate.
17 Serve the plates and the mugs of hot chocolate on the table. This could be served on a tray as a TV snack, or a supper snack or for 'elevenses'.

Let's clear away

1 Stack all the things for washing-up, near the sink.
2 Wipe over the table, the work-top and stove with a dish-cloth. Then rinse the dish-cloth and squeeze out the water.

3 Fill a bowl with warm water in which you can comfortably hold your hands. Squeeze in a little washing-up liquid. All sticky foods, like sugar and grease need hot water to get them clean. All foods made of milk or egg come clean more easily if soaked first in cold water. This is why soaking pans and dishes in the right temperature water makes the job of washing-up easier.

4 The order in which you should wash up is always from the cleanest to the dirtiest items. Today, you wash first the cutlery, then the plates and the mugs, then the bread-board. Then get a pan scrubber to clean the saucepan and the grill-pan.

5 When you have finished, wipe round the bowl with the dish-cloth, rinse under the tap, wring out the water and wipe the bowl dry.

6 Wipe up with a clean tea towel and put away tidily.

Let's Make Chocolate Crunchies

Makes 8

Food to collect

1 level tablespoon syrup
1 level tablespoon sugar
2 equal portions margarine (see page 9)
1½ teacupsful cornflakes
1 rounded tablespoon cocoa

Equipment to collect

1 saucepan with a thick base
1 basin in which to put corn-flakes
1 basin or cup in which to put cocoa
1 wooden spoon
1 tablespoon
1 dessertspoon
1 baking tray
8 paper cake cases
heat-proof mat for work-top

Preparation

* Wash your hands. Put on your apron.

* Collect the food and equipment. Put neatly on the work-top.
* Spread out the paper cake cases on the baking tray.

Method of work

1 Measure out the syrup, sugar and margarine. Make sure you use a clean spoon each time. Put all three in the saucepan and take it to the stove.

2 Light a ring or turn on a hot-plate and set the heat at LOW or on the lowest number.

3 You must leave the contents of the pan until they slowly turn to liquid. The sugar will dissolve and the margarine will melt.

4 Meanwhile measure out the cornflakes and tip into the basin. Then measure out the cocoa and leave in another basin, or a cup.

5 When you think the mixture in the pan is ready, give it a good stir with a wooden spoon to make sure there are no grains of sugar left on the bottom of the pan. Then turn off the heat.

6 Put the pan on a heat-proof mat on the work-top, although the mixture inside should only be WARM, not hot.

7 First put in the cocoa and stir it in with a wooden spoon.

8 Then add the cornflakes and gently stir until the chocolate mixture coats every flake.

9 Put a heaped dessertspoon of mixture into each paper case.

10 Use up all the mixture. Then stand the pan in hot water to soak.

11 The chocolate crunchies are now finished but you must leave them to cool and become firm.

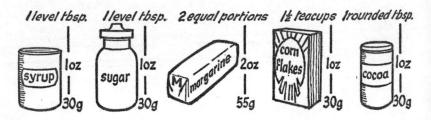

1 level tbsp.   1 level tbsp.   2 equal portions   1½ teacups   1 rounded tbsp.

syrup 1oz 30g   sugar 1oz 30g   margarine 2oz 55g   corn Flakes 1oz 30g   cocoa 1oz 30g

12 Whilst you are waiting for them to set, you can clear away.

13 Stack the dirty things first. Put away the rest of the food. Wipe over the work-top and stove. Wash up in hot water. Do you remember the right order? (see page 21) When you have finished washing, wipe the bowl dry with a clean dish-cloth and make sure you leave a clean sink. Now wipe up and put everything away tidily.

Before you are tempted to taste your cakes, read on.

Let's Make some Tea so we can eat the Cakes

For 2

Food to collect
The tea caddy

Equipment to collect
a kettle
1 tray

Preparation
* Wash your hands. Put on your apron.
* Collect the tea caddy and the kettle. Put on the work-top.
* Set the tray as shown.

For the tray

2 teacups, saucers and spoons
1 plate for cakes
sugar bowl and spoon
milk in a small jug

PUT NEAR THE KETTLE
a teapot and cosy

Method of work
1 Fill the kettle and put it on.

2 Pour hot water in the teapot and stand to warm through, this is called 'warming the pot'.

3 Whilst you are waiting for the kettle to boil, set the chocolate crunchies on a plate. A paper doily on the plate will make the cakes look more attractive.

4 When the water is nearly boiling, tip out the water that warmed the pot and put into the pot 3 teaspoonsful of tea. The rule for the amount of tea to put in the pot, is one teaspoon of tea for each person plus one for the pot. But if you know that someone likes strong tea or that you are going to offer 'second cups of tea' then put in two teaspoonsful of tea for the pot.

5 Stand the pot near the kettle. When the water boils, turn off the heat and pour in just enough water for two cups. Put the cosy over the pot and allow it to brew for at least three minutes before pouring out. Stand the pot on the tray.

6 Whilst you are waiting for the tea to brew, put the milk in the cups. Usually everyone sugars his or her own tea because some people like a lot, some a little and some none at all. If you have visitors to the house, you should ask them if they take milk in their tea as some people like it black (no milk) and others like a slice of lemon instead of milk.

7 Now pour the tea, and offer the teacup and saucer, then the sugar basin to your companion.

8 And, of course, the cakes!

9 If you want a second cup of tea, boil up the kettle again and pour some water into the teapot, put on the cosy and again allow to brew. Tea can be served any time your friends come to see you or during the afternoon.

Breakfasts

This is the meal that is going to take you through the morning whether at work or at play. It should be quick to prepare so the simplest dishes are the best choice.

A breakfast of toast or bread, butter and marmalade, tea or coffee is very easy to prepare but it is not going to do your body nearly so much good as a breakfast that includes ONE main food from the following list:

a meat dish
a fish dish
a cheese dish
an egg dish

This, with a cereal first and toast or bread and butter, marmalade or honey and a drink with milk in it. Fresh fruit, especially oranges, grapefruit, lemons or blackcurrants, taken either as a prepared drink or eaten as whole fruit will also help to keep you very fit and well.

In the winter months you need a more filling breakfast than in the summer time in order to keep out the cold. Think of serving porridge instead of breakfast cereals to start the day.

Orange Juice : Cold Meat : Toast and Honey : Tea

For 2

Food to collect

1 small carton frozen orange juice
4 slices cold meat
2 tomatoes
a few sprigs parsley, if possible
4 slices thick bread for toast
3 teaspoons tea from caddy

Equipment to collect

1 jug
1 toast rack
2 dessert plates
1 chopping board or bread board
1 teapot and cosy
a kettle

Preparation

* Wash your hands. Put on your apron.
* Collect the food and equipment. Put neatly on the work-top.
* Hold the stalks of parsley and rinse the sprigs under water. SHAKE THEM WELL.
* Set table as shown.

For the table

2 place-mats or a cloth
2 paper serviettes
2 knives and forks
2 dessert knives
2 tea plates
2 teacups, saucers and spoons
2 glasses
sugar bowl and spoon
milk jug
butter dish and knife
honeypot and spoon
pepper, salt, mustard
teapot stand

Method of work

1 Fill the kettle and put it on to boil.
2 Warm the pot.
3 Heat the grill.
4 Pour the orange juice into the jug. Read the carton to find out how much water to add. Then stand the jug on the table.
5 Cut the tomatoes into quarters on the chopping board. The sharpest edge of the knife must be kept downwards. Put the quarters on the plates.

6 Arrange the slices of meat on each plate.

7 Take the stalks off the parsley, put the sprigs only in the centre of each plate. This touch of colour is called a garnish.

8 Put the toast on the grid and place it under the grill heat.

9 Make the tea when the water in the kettle is really BOILING. Remember the cosy. And the teapot stand for the table.

10 Does the toast need turning?

11 When the toast is a golden brown both sides, turn off the heat, put the toast in the rack, take it to the table and serve it hot.

Whilst you are eating your breakfast think whether or not the preparations went smoothly. If everything wanted attention at the same time the only answer is to move the cooking from the source of heat. For example, you can take the grill-pan out from the heat and leave it on the grill flap or a cool part of the top of the stove if the toast looks as if it is browning. You can turn the kettle off or take it off the heat if it is boiling. It can always be reboiled again later. If you have milk near to boiling in a saucepan then lift it off the heat on to a cool part of the stove until you need to use it.

Grapefruit Juice : Boiled Eggs : Toast and Marmalade : Tea

For 2

Food to collect

1 small carton frozen grapefruit juice

2 eggs

4 slices thick bread for toast

3 teaspoons tea from caddy

Equipment to collect

1 jug

1 toast rack

a saucepan to boil the eggs

1 tablespoon

1 basin

a teapot and cosy.

a kettle

Preparation

* Wash your hands. Put on your apron.
* Collect the food and equipment. Put neatly on the work-top.
* Set the table as shown.

For the table

2 place-mats or a cloth
2 dessert knives
4 tea plates
2 egg cups and spoons
2 teacups, saucers and spoons
2 glasses
sugar bowl and spoon
milk jug
butter dish and knife
marmalade pot and spoon
salt
teapot stand
2 paper serviettes

Method of work

1 Make the grapefruit juice in the jug, following the instructions on the carton. Stand it on the table.
2 Half fill a saucepan with water, put it on the stove and light a ring under it or turn on a hot plate. Set the heat at MEDIUM.
3 Heat the grill.
4 Fill the kettle with water and put it on.
5 When the water in the saucepan is gently bubbling, carry the eggs in the basin to the stove. Then gently lower each egg into the water on a tablespoon. Look at the clock.

For SOFT-boiled eggs allow 3–4 minutes once the water boils again.

For HARD-boiled eggs allow 8–10 minutes once the water boils again.
6 Put the toast under the grill.

7 Warm the pot.

8 Stay at the stove to watch the toast and time the eggs. When the kettle boils turn it off or take it off and make the tea. Put the teapot on the table.

9 When the toast is golden both sides, turn off the grill, put the toast in the rack and leave in a warm place.

10 When the eggs are cooked, turn off the heat below the pan. Lift out each egg with a tablespoon and put in a basin.

11 Carry the eggs and toast to the table. Put the eggs in their cups.

Cereal : Grilled Bacon, Sausage and Tomato : Bread Rolls : Tea

For 2

Food to collect

4 rashers bacon
2 tomatoes
2 sausages
2 bread rolls
3 teaspoons tea from the caddy

Equipment to collect

kitchen scissors
a vegetable knife
a chopping board
1 plate for bacon, sausages and tomatoes
1 fork
grill-pan
1 teapot and cosy
a kettle

Preparation

* Wash your hands. Put on your apron.
* Collect the food and equipment. Put neatly on the work-top.
* Set the table as shown on the next page.

For the table

2 place-mats or a cloth
2 knives and forks

2 dessert knives
2 dishes for cornflakes
2 dessert spoons
2 tea plates
2 paper serviettes
2 teacups, saucers and spoons
a packet of cornflakes
sugar bowl and spoon
milk jug
butter dish and knife
salt and pepper
teapot stand
2 table-mats

PUT TO WARM
2 dessert plates

Method of work

1 Heat the grill.
2 Warm the pot. Put the kettle on to boil.
3 With a fork, prick the sausages here and there. If you do not, they may burst their skins as the inside gets hot. Remember that as things get hot they get bigger in size or expand. At some stage, the hot sausage may be making the skin around it feel tight. By pricking the skin you will just ease it to allow it to get bigger with the meat inside. Skinless sausages do not need pricking. Put the sausages under the grill.
4 If the bacon has a rind on it, cut it off. Snip the fat edge here and there to prevent it from curling up with the heat.

5 Turn each tomato on its side and cut in half on the chopping board. Remember to use the sharp edge of the knife downwards, sawing backwards and forwards.
6 Put the bacon and tomatoes under the grill. Turn the sausages over to get even browning.
7 Make the tea and stand the pot on the table. Put the rolls on to tea plates.
8 When the bacon fat is a golden brown on one side, turn it over.
9 Remember that you are going to eat the cornflakes first, so you will want to keep the bacon, sausages and tomatoes warm. If you do not have a warming drawer or compartment, then just before they are ready, turn the grill to LOW or the lowest number marked, and put the grill-pan as far away from the heat as possible. Eat your cornflakes and by the time you have finished and stacked the dishes and spoons by the sink, the grilled breakfast will be just right to serve on to the plates. Turn off the grill.

Porridge : Kippers : Bread and Butter : Marmalade : Tea

For 2

Food to collect	**Equipment to collect**
a packet of instant porridge	1 saucepan large enough for kippers
1 teacupful milk	
a pinch of salt	a milk saucepan
a small packet of frozen 'boil in a bag' kipper fillets	a bread board
	a butter knife
4 slices of bread	a colander
butter	a fish slice
3 teaspoons tea from caddy	a pair of kitchen scissors
	a teapot and cosy
	a kettle

Preparation

* Wash your hands. Put on your apron.
* Collect the food and equipment. Put neatly on the work-top. Keep the plate for bread and butter on the table for the moment.
* Set the table as shown.

For the table

2 place-mats or a cloth
2 paper serviettes
2 fish knives and forks
2 dessert knives
2 dessert spoons
2 tea plates
2 teacups, saucers and spoons
a bread and butter plate
sugar bowl and spoon
milk jug
marmalade pot and spoon
vinegar
teapot stand
2 table mats

PUT TO WARM
2 bowls for porridge
2 dessert plates

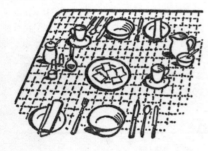

Method of work

1 Before you fill the saucepan, make sure the bag of kippers fits into it. Once you have tried, take them out. Fill the saucepan three-quarters full with water. Set the heat on HIGH or the highest number marked. The saucepan lid fitted over the saucepan will make the water boil more quickly because it keeps all the hot steam inside, stopping it from being carried away by the cold air outside.

2 Butter the bread on the board. Arrange on the plate and put on the table.

3 Warm the pot. Fill and put the kettle on to boil.

4 When the water in the saucepan is boiling, carefully lower the packet into the water. Put the lid back half-way. Look at the clock. Time the kippers with the instructions on the packet. Turn the heat down to MEDIUM.

5 Put the porridge bowls on the work-top. Measure out the porridge following the instructions on the packet.

6 Measure out the milk and put in the saucepan. Put on to simmer. Set the heat at MEDIUM.

7 Make the tea when the kettle is boiling and put the pot on the table.

8 When the milk simmers (remember you look for tiny bubbles around the sides of the saucepan and beginning to spread to the centre) turn off the heat and take carefully to the work-top. Pour a little milk on to each bowl and then put the pan on a stand while you stir with a tablespoon. When it is smooth add the remaining milk to the bowls. Add a pinch of salt to each bowl. Then put the pan to soak in cold water.

9 Serve and start to eat the porridge. You will enjoy milk and sugar added to it.
When you have eaten the porridge, check the time to see if the kippers are ready.

10 Stack the porridge bowls by the sink.

11 Turn the heat off from under the kippers, take the saucepan to the sink and pour through the colander.

12 Run a *little* cold water on to the bag so you are able to handle it.

13 Set the warm plates on the work-top. Put the packet on the board.

14 Cut the edge of the packet all round with the kitchen scissors. Lift out the kipper fillets with a fish slice and serve on the plates.

Elevenses

This is just a small refreshment to help you on to lunchtime. It must not be another meal. If it is going to fill you up so that you do not want any lunch then it is best left out altogether.

If elevenses are going to be served, then as with all other food, do so attractively. Even cups of coffee and biscuits look much better if set on a nice clean tray with a well-ironed tray-cloth and matching china. If you are going to serve biscuits, scones or cakes at any time, then a paper doily on the plate will make them look pretty.

Coffee is usually served mid-morning but other milk drinks or tea can be made just as well. It depends on what you prefer.

Instant Coffee

For 2

Food to collect	**Equipment to collect**
jar of instant coffee	1 milk saucepan
about a teacup of milk	a kettle
	1 teacup
	1 teaspoon

Preparation
* Wash your hands. Put on your apron.
* Set the tray as shown.
* Put the two teacups you are going to drink from, on the work-top.

For the tray
sugar bowl and spoon
2 saucers and spoons
2 teacups to be put on work-top

Method of work

1 Fill the kettle with cold water.
2 Put it on to boil.
3 Rinse out a milk saucepan with cold water. This will help to stop the hot milk from sticking to the pan. Now put the milk into the pan.
4 Put on a low heat to WARM through but not to boil.
5 Into each cup put about 1 teaspoon of coffee. The amount really depends on how strong or weak you like it.
6 When the milk begins to show very tiny bubbles around the edge of the pan, turn off the heat, as it is simmering.
7 Take the pan to the work-top and pour half the milk into each cup.
8 Put the saucepan into cold water to soak.
9 When the kettle boils, turn off, and pour the boiling water on to the milk and coffee. Gently stir round with a teaspoon to make sure the coffee is dissolved and the milk and water is mixed.
10 Carry the cups carefully to the saucers on the tray. You should have two clean teaspoons there.

This is coffee made with half milk and half water. Some people may like coffee made with all water, then it is called black coffee. Young children may like it made with all milk. If you are in any doubt as to how people like to drink coffee, you can always ask them before making it.

Flapjacks

Makes 8

Food to collect

2 level tablespoons syrup
6 level tablespoons brown sugar
3 equal portions margarine (see page 9)
6 heaped tablespoons rolled oats
a squeeze of 'jiffi' lemon
a pinch of salt
a little lard or cooking oil

Equipment to collect

a sandwich tin
a baking tray
a thick-based saucepan
1 tablespoon
1 teaspoon
1 wooden spoon
1 ordinary knife
1 mixing bowl
greaseproof paper
a pencil
a pair of paper scissors

Preparation

* Wash your hands. Put on your apron.
* Collect the food and equipment. Put neatly on the work-top.
* Put the oven on at R3/160°C/325°F. Put a shelf at the middle of the oven. Make sure there is an oven-cloth nearby.

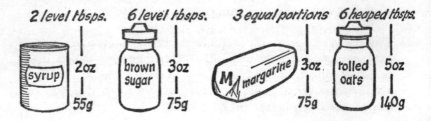

2 level tbsps. — syrup — 2oz — 55g
6 level tbsps. — brown sugar — 3oz — 75g
3 equal portions — margarine — 3oz — 75g
6 heaped tbsps. — rolled oats — 5oz — 140g

* Stand the base of the sandwich tin on a corner of the greaseproof paper, draw round it with a pencil. Cut out on the pencil line.
* Rub a little lard or brush with a little oil over the inside of the sandwich tin. Put the paper circle into the tin and grease with lard or oil over the paper.

Method of work

1 Measure out the syrup using a knife to level it off in the bowl of the spoon. Use a clean spoon to measure out the brown sugar. Measure out the margarine and put all three, syrup, sugar and margarine, into a saucepan. Put on a LOW heat or the lowest number marked, until the margarine has melted and all the sugar dissolved.

2 Whilst you are waiting, measure out the oats and the salt and the lemon juice and put them all into a mixing bowl.

3 When the mixture in the saucepan is ready, stir round with a wooden spoon to make sure everything is runny, then stand the pan on the work-top on a heat-proof mat.

4 Add the oats and salt with the tablespoon and then stir very well with the wooden spoon.

5 Put the mixture into the prepared tin. The greased paper will help to stop the mixture from sticking to the tin when it is cooked.

6 Stand the tin on a baking tray and put on the middle shelf in the oven. Shut the door tightly.

7 Look at the clock. The flapjacks should be ready in 15–20 minutes. Meanwhile, stack all the dishes neatly and wipe over the work-top with a clean dish-cloth. Wash up, wipe up and put the equipment and remaining food away tidily.

8 When cooked, stand the tin on top of the oven to cool. As the mixture will still be soft, cut into 8 triangles. Leave in the tin to crisp and cool before turning out. Do not forget to turn off the oven.

Gingernuts

Makes 18

Food to collect	**Equipment to collect**
4 heaped tablespoons plain flour	a baking tray
1 rounded teaspoon ground ginger	a thick-based saucepan
	1 tablespoon
½ level teaspoon baking powder	1 teaspoon
2 level tablespoons brown sugar	1 wooden spoon
2 equal portions margarine (see page 9)	1 knife
	1 mixing bowl
3 level tablespoons syrup	1 sieve
a little lard or cooking oil	1 palette knife

Preparation
* Wash your hands. Put on your apron.
* Collect the food and equipment. Put neatly on the work-top.
* Put the oven on at R3/160°C/325°F. Put a shelf at the middle of the oven. Make sure there is an oven-cloth nearby.
* Rub a little lard, or brush a little oil, over the baking tray.

Method of work
1 Measure out the flour, baking powder and ground ginger. Sieve them into a mixing bowl. Make a 'well' or hole in the centre of these ingredients.

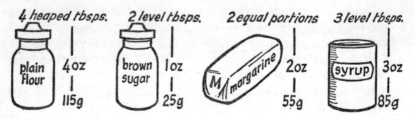

4 heaped tbsps. plain flour 4oz 115g

2 level tbsps. brown sugar 1oz 25g

2 equal portions margarine 2oz 55g

3 level tbsps. syrup 3oz 85g

2 Measure out the sugar, margarine and syrup, using a clean spoon each time, and put these three into a saucepan.

3 Put the saucepan on a LOW heat or on the lowest number marked until the margarine has melted and the sugar dissolved.

4 When the mixture in the saucepan is ready, stir round with a wooden spoon to make sure everything is runny, then put on a heat-proof mat on your work-top.

5 Pour the mixture into the 'well' in the flour. Make sure you scrape the saucepan clean with the wooden spoon.

6 Then quickly stir all the ingredients together until they are thoroughly mixed.

7 Stop for one moment to put your saucepan to soak in hot water.

8 Take a teaspoon of the mixture, roll it in your hands to form a ball. Put it on the baking tray.

9 Repeat this for all the biscuits but you must leave $1\frac{1}{2}$ in/4 cm between each biscuit so they can spread out once they start to cook.

10 Use up all the mixture from the bowl. Then flatten each ball slightly with your flat hand.

11 Put the biscuits on the middle shelf in the oven.

12 Look at the time. They should be ready in 15–20 minutes. Meanwhile stack all the washing-up neatly, then wipe over the work-top with a clean dish-cloth. Wash and wipe up. Put the equipment and remaining food away tidily.

13 At the end of the cooking time, look in the oven, and if the biscuits smell good and look a golden brown then put them on top of the oven. They should look quite dry in appearance.

14 The biscuits will still be soft to touch because they only crisp on cooling. You can cool them more quickly by putting them on a cooling tray or a wire rack – the grid of the grill-pan will do. Lift each biscuit on a palette knife. Make sure the cooling tray is placed next to the biscuits so you have not far to shift them.

15 Do not forget to turn off the oven or to wash up the baking tray.

Shortbread

Makes 8

Food to collect

6 heaped tablespoons plain flour
a pinch of salt
4 equal portions margarine or
butter (see page 9)
4 level tablespoons castor sugar
a little lard or cooking oil

Equipment to collect

a sandwich tin
a baking tray
1 tablespoon
1 ordinary knife
1 fork
a mixing bowl
a sieve
greaseproof paper
a pencil
a pair of paper scissors
a plate for the sugar

Preparation
* Wash your hands. Put on your apron.
* Collect the food and equipment. Put neatly on the work-top.
* Put the oven on at R3/160°C/325°F. Put a shelf at the middle
of the oven. Make sure there is an oven-cloth nearby.
* Stand the base of the sandwich tin on a corner of the greaseproof
paper, draw round it with a pencil. Cut out on the pencil line.
* Rub a little lard, or brush with a little oil, over the inside of the
sandwich tin. Put the paper circle into the tin and grease over
the paper.

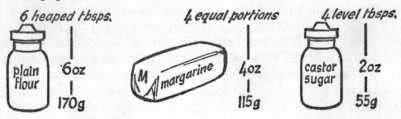

6 heaped tbsps. plain flour 6oz 170g

4 equal portions margarine 4oz 115g

4 level tbsps. castor sugar 2oz 55g

Method of work

1 Measure out the ingredients. Sieve the flour and salt into a mixing bowl.

2 Put the margarine into the mixing bowl and cut it up with a knife.

3 With the tips of your fingers, rub the margarine into the flour until it looks like breadcrumbs.

4 Add the sugar and mix it with a knife.

5 Collect the mixture together with your hands into a large ball.

6 When you have it bound together, put into the prepared sandwich tin and with your knuckles press the mixture down until it fits the sandwich tin.

7 To get a flat top, you can smooth over with a palette knife.

8 Mark into 8 equal triangles, then go back over the marking lines and cut through to the tin.

9 Prick all over the shortbread with a fork. This helps to let out the air that may have got into the mixture. As air gets warm it expands or gets bigger thus making cakes or scones rise. We want the biscuits to stay flat so the answer is to prick.

10 Put on a baking tray and put into the oven, on the middle shelf.

11 Look at the time. It will take about 1 hour.

12 Meanwhile wash and wipe up and put everything away tidily.

13 When cooked the shortbread should look a pale biscuit colour, and quite dry. Stand it on top of the stove and again cut through the triangles you had cut before, as during cooking they may have joined up. Then leave in the tin to cool before turning out. Did you remember to turn off the oven?

Cheese Scones

Makes 6

Food to collect
4 heaped tablespoons self-raising flour
a pinch of salt
1 equal portion margarine (see page 9)
5 tablespoons milk
3 level tablespoons grated cheese
a little lard or cooking oil

Equipment to collect
a baking tray
1 tablespoon
1 teaspoon
1 knife
a mixing bowl
a saucer
a sieve
a cheese-grater
a pastry brush

Preparation
* Wash your hands. Put on your apron.
* Collect the food and equipment. Put neatly on the work-top.

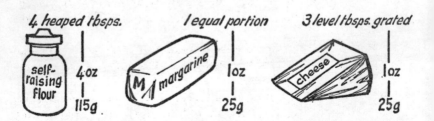

4 heaped tbsps.   1 equal portion   3 level tbsps. grated
self-raising flour   4 oz   115g   margarine   1 oz   25g   cheese   1 oz   25g

* Put the oven on at R8/235°C/450°F. Put a shelf at the top of the oven. Make sure there is an oven-cloth nearby.
* Rub a little lard or brush a little oil over a baking tray.
* Grate the cheese on to a plate – dry cheese will be best.
* Put 1 tablespoon of milk into a saucer. This will be brushed on top of the scones just before going into the oven; it will make them a shiny golden colour and it is called a 'glaze'.

Method of work

1 Sieve the flour and salt into the mixing bowl.
2 Put the margarine into the bowl and rub it into the flour with your fingertips until it disappears.
3 Add the grated cheese.
4 Make a 'well' in the flour.
5 Put in the remaining 4 tablespoons of milk and mix round with a knife. Mix until it is smooth. This mixture is now called a dough.
6 Collect the dough together with your hand until it comes to a ball.
7 Put the dough in the centre of your baking tray and flatten into a round about $\frac{3}{4}$ in/2 cm thick. You can use a saucer as a guide for the size.
8 Mark out the top into 6 triangles and cut through.
9 Brush over the top of the scones with milk glaze that you have prepared.
10 Put the scones in the oven on the top shelf. Look at the clock. The scones should be ready in 7–10 minutes, so keep wide awake.
11 You can start to stack the equipment and wipe over the work-top. See how much of the washing and wiping up you can get finished.
12 When ready the scones should have risen. You should be able to smell the cheese. They should be quite dry looking and nicely brown on top.

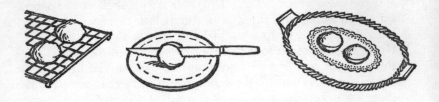

13 Put the baking tray on top of the stove and after it has cooled a little, take off the scones and put on a wire rack. Do not forget to turn off the oven.

Serve the scones cut in half and buttered.

They can also be served at teatime with a slice of tomato in the middle.

Lunches

Some families have their main meal at mid-day and this is called lunch.

Others have theirs in the evening and this is called dinner. It does depend on the time when all the family are at home and can sit down together. Also when the one who cooks the meal has most time to do so.

Whether the main meal is mid-day or in the evening, it should be a good substantial meal to satisfy your hunger.

The main course is usually built around meat or fish. Then a green vegetable or a salad should be added. Sometimes a second vegetable is added such as carrots, turnips or parsnips. There should also be a portion of potatoes or savoury rice or spaghetti or noodles.

Flavourings in the form of gravies, stuffings, sauces and garnishes all help to make the meal look more colourful and attractive, and most important of all, to taste better.

The second course is usually sweet and in the form of fruit or a milk type dessert, or in winter, a pudding.

Many people like to finish their main meal with coffee and cheese and biscuits.

An Easy Lunch of Cold Meat, Salad and Crisps : Fruit Crumble and Cream

For 2

Food to collect for salad
4 slices of ham or tongue or pork
2 tomatoes

Equipment to collect
an *old* newspaper for waste
a dish, bowl or plate for salad

about 6 lettuce leaves or 1
    bunch of watercress
¼ cucumber or 1 stick of celery
a few spring onions, if possible
either salad cream or French
    dressing
pickles or chutney
2 bags of crisps

Food to collect for fruit crumble

enough fruit to come ¾ the way
    in a pint or ½ litre dish (use
    apricots or plums or goose-
    berries or rhubarb)
6 level tablespoons granulated
    sugar
2 tablespoons water

Crumble mixture

4 heaped tablespoons plain flour
2 equal portions margarine (see
    page 9)
4 level tablespoons granulated
    sugar

Cream

a small tub, jar or tin of cream

2 dinner plates
1 vegetable knife
1 chopping board
1 clean tea towel
1 small jug to put salad cream
    or French dressing in
1 small dish to put pickles or
    chutney in and small spoon
1 dish for crisps
2 serving spoons for salad
1 serving or tablespoon for
    crisps
a deep, heat-proof dish (1 pt/½l)
    for crumble
a small dish and spoon
    for cream
a colander to wash fruit
a baking tray
an ordinary knife
1 tablespoon
1 palette knife
a mixing bowl
kitchen scissors
a sieve

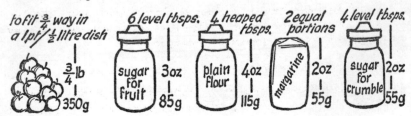

to fit ¾ way in a 1pt/½ litre dish — ¾ lb / 350g

6 level tbsps. sugar for fruit — 3oz / 85g

4 heaped tbsps. plain flour — 4oz / 115g

2 equal portions margarine — 2oz / 55g

4 level tbsps. sugar for crumble — 2oz / 55g

Preparation

* Wash your hands. Put on your apron.
* Collect the food and equipment. Put neatly on the work-top.
* Put the oven on at R6/205°C/400°F. Put a shelf in the middle of the oven. Make sure there is an oven-cloth nearby.
* Spread out the newspaper to collect any bits you may want to throw away.

Method of work

Preparing the lettuce:

1 Take the lettuce and look at it carefully. Some of the outside leaves may have to be thrown away because they are brown and bruised, but try not to be wasteful. All the leaves will turn like this unless you handle them very gently.

2 With your hand pull off each leaf at the base. Do not cut the leaves with a knife, otherwise they will turn brown. The parts you are going to throw away, put in the newspaper. Those you are going to eat, put on a plate.

3 Spread a clean tea towel on your work-top. Fill a bowl with cold water and wash each leaf in it very carefully. You will have to look closely to make sure all the bits of earth and insects have gone. Then shake off any drops of water over the bowl and put on the tea towel. Repeat with each leaf. Put the leaves in one half of the tea towel, fold over the other half. Leave the leaves to dry for as long as you can.

Preparing the watercress:

4 Hold the watercress by the long stalks and wash under the tap. Spread the leaves out on to the clean tea towel, pick out any yellow or brown parts and leave to dry.

Preparing the fruit crumble:

5 *Apricots or plums:* prepare by taking off any stalks or leaves. Make sure there are no bad spots, if so, cut round with a

vegetable knife on the chopping board. Put in the colander and wash under the tap. Take back to the chopping board and using a vegetable knife, cut each fruit in half to take out the stone. Put the halved fruit in the heat-proof dish.

Gooseberries: prepare by snipping off the top stalk and hairy tail with a pair of scissors. Then put in a colander and wash under the tap. Put into the heat-proof dish.

Rhubarb: prepare by taking off any leaves and throwing them away in newspaper. If there is any white showing at the base of the stem cut it off on your chopping board, this is the part that goes into the earth. Wash the stems very well under the tap, then take to the chopping board to cut into 1 inch or 2·5 cm lengths. This can be done by using a vegetable knife or with a pair of kitchen scissors. Then put in the dish.

6 Sprinkle the sugar over the fruit. Carefully mix the sugar in, so that it does not all remain on top.

7 Wipe down the work-top and stack the used equipment near the sink.

8 Measure out the ingredients for the crumble.

9 Sieve the flour into the bowl, add the sugar and margarine.

10 With an ordinary knife, cut up the margarine in the mixing bowl.

11 With the fingertips, rub the margarine into the flour and sugar until it looks like fine breadcrumbs. Shake the bowl to make sure you have not missed any big lumps of margarine.

12 Using a tablespoon, put the crumble over the fruit in the dish. Cover all the fruit.

13 Wipe the edge of the dish with a clean cloth otherwise the mixture that cooks on to the dish will be difficult to get off later and it will also spoil the appearance of the dish when served.

14 Stand the dish on a baking tray and put on to the middle shelf of the oven. It should take 35–40 minutes to soften the fruit and cook the crumble.

15 Wipe down the work-top and wash up the dirty equipment.

Preparation of cucumber or celery, and spring onions:

16 Take the cucumber or celery and wash it. With a vegetable knife cut down on to a chopping board. The cucumber must be sliced as thinly as you can get it otherwise it might be indigestible. The celery can be cut up into larger pieces, up to 1 in or 2·5 cm long. These can be placed on the clean tea towel with the lettuce.

17 Put the spring onions on the chopping board and cut off the hairy roots. Throw these bits away in the newspaper. Now take off the first layer of onion skin. This is the skin that might have gone a little brown but the under layers should be nice and white. You can leave the green hollow stems at the top of the onion because these have a mild onion flavour. If the tip is yellow cut it off and put in the newspaper.

Preparation of tomatoes:

18 Wash and wipe the tomatoes carefully. Cut them into quarters on the chopping board.

Putting the salad together:

19 Now you have prepared the different parts of the salad you can mix it together. If you want to arrange the salad to make it look pretty, choose a large flat plate or shallow dish. If you do not want to arrange the salad, then a deeper bowl is better. Whichever you choose, make sure that you start with the lettuce or watercress as these are the largest shapes. When the salad is finished, make sure that nothing hangs over the side of the plate, dish or bowl.

20 Into a small jug or sauceboat put a little salad cream or French dressing to serve with the salad. This is a mixture of olive oil and vinegar with salt, pepper and mustard added.
Into a small dish put a little chutney or pickle. A small spoon or pickle fork will be needed. Tip the crisps into a dish and do not eat them yet!

Open the cream and put it into a small jug or a small dish with a spoon.

21 PUT TO WARM
2 dessert plates for the crumble

Set the table with:

2 place-mats or a cloth	the dish of crisps
2 paper serviettes	a table-mat for the crumble
2 dinner knives and forks	the jug of salad cream or French
2 dessert forks and spoons	dressing
4 serving or tablespoons	the dish of chutney or pickle and
pepper, salt and mustard	spoon
the bowl or plate of salad	the jug of cream and spoon

22 Look at the time. Should the crumble be cooked yet? If so it should look crisp and a golden brown on top. Perhaps you are using a heat-proof, glass dish and therefore can see the fruit, if so it should look soft and juicy.
When cooked, turn the oven down to R$\frac{1}{4}$/90°C/200°F and leave the door slightly ajar. This will keep the crumble warm.

23 Before sitting down to eat, you should tidy the kitchen and wipe over the work-top. After you have eaten, wash up, wipe up and put away all the equipment you have used.

Beef, Potato and Cheese Pie : Spinach : Baked Apples

For 2

Food to collect for the pie
4 slices corned beef
1 packet dried potatoes to
serve 2–3

Equipment to collect
a deep, heat-proof dish
2 saucepans
a cheese-grater

4 heaped tablespoons grated
  cheese
4 tomatoes
a little butter or margarine

**Food to collect for the
  spinach**

1 small frozen packet spinach
a knob of butter
salt

**Food to collect for baked
  apples**

2 cooking apples
1 tablespoon of sugar or
  syrup
2 tablespoons water
1 tablespoon of currants,
  sultanas or dates, if liked

a plate
a wooden spoon
1 tablespoon
an apple corer or a vegetable
  peeler
1 palette knife
1 vegetable knife
a chopping board
a shallow, heat-proof dish
2 baking trays
newspaper
a sieve or colander

Preparation

* Wash your hands. Put on your apron.
* Collect the food and equipment. Put neatly on the work-top.
* Put oven on at R6/205°C/400°F. Put a shelf at the top of the
  oven for the pie in the deep dish to go on. Put a shelf in the
  middle of the oven for the apples in the shallow dish to go on.
  Make sure there is an oven-cloth nearby.
* Grate the cheese on to a plate.
* Rub a little butter or margarine around the inside of the
  deep, heat-proof dish.

Method of work

Preparing the baked apples:

1 Take the two apples, which should be about the same size,
  and thoroughly wash them in hot water.

51

2 Stand on the chopping board to take out the core with either an apple corer or a vegetable peeler. Put the corer or peeler into the apple just by the stalk and ease it gently half-way down the apple, twist it round the core and then withdraw the corer or peeler. Turn the apple up the other way and again put the corer or peeler into the centre of the apple. Push it down half-way, twist it round the core and then pull out once more. You can now look inside the apple to see if all the core is out, if not make a third attempt.

3 Then with the very tip of the vegetable knife, cut the skin of the apple round the middle as shown. This is done for the same reason as pricking sausages, to stop the inside of the hot apple from splitting its skin.

When the apples have become hot in the oven you will see a gap in the middle of the apple because the inside has got bigger.

4 When both apples have been cored and cut round the middle, put them in the shallow dish. Fill the middle of each apple with two teaspoons of sugar or syrup. Then add currants, sultanas or dates.

5 Lastly, spoon over each apple a tablespoon of water. Stand the dish on a baking tray and put on the middle shelf of the oven for about 30–40 minutes. When cooked the apples should be soft through to the centre but still in shape.

6 Wipe down the work-top and wash up the used equipment.

Preparing the beef, potato and cheese pie:

7 Cut the tomatoes into slices on the chopping board, see diagram on page 30. Read the instructions on the packet of dried potatoes. Measure out the water into a saucepan and put on to boil.

8 Use a palette knife to lay out the slices of corned beef on the chopping board, if there are likely to be flies about cover with a clean cloth or a large plate.

9 When the water for the potatoes comes to the boil, take it off the heat and put on a heat-proof mat on the work-top. Add the dried potatoes and a knob of butter. Stir very well until thick and smooth.

10 Put into the potatoes about three-quarters of the cheese you have grated. Save the remaining quarter for the top of the pie.

11 Stir the cheese and potato mixture together, then put half the potatoes in the deep, heatproof dish. Now add a layer of the tomato slices. On to the tomatoes sprinkle a pinch of salt, then cover with the slices of corned beef. Add the rest of the potatoes and smooth them over with a palette knife. Finally, sprinkle over the grated cheese you have saved.

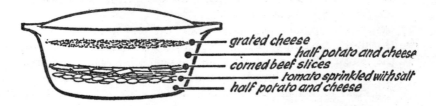

grated cheese
half potato and cheese
corned beef slices
tomato sprinkled with salt
half potato and cheese

12 Stand the dish on a baking tray and put on the top shelf of the oven for 20–25 minutes.

13 Wipe down the work-top and wash and wipe up the equipment.

14 PUT TO WARM
2 dinner plates
1 vegetable dish for the spinacn
2 dessert plates or dishes for the baked apples

Set the table with:

2 place-mats or a cloth	2 dessert spoons and forks
2 paper serviettes	3 serving or tablespoons
2 dinner knives and forks	pepper, salt and mustard
	2 table-mats for the hot dishes

15 The spinach will only take 3–6 minutes to cook therefore the other dishes should be almost cooked before putting it on. Take the packet of spinach and read the instructions. Then follow them carefully. Measure out the water into a saucepan and put on to boil. If the spinach is already thawed out (that means no ice is left), then it will only take 3 minutes in cooking time. If the spinach is still frozen, then it will take up to 6 minutes simmering once the ice has thawed in the saucepan.

16 Whilst the spinach is simmering, open the oven door and take out each dish in turn to test whether it is cooked. The apples should be soft and juicy. The pie should be heated through and a golden brown on top. If the pie is heated through but still a pale colour, heat up the grill and stand it under the grill heat for a few minutes until a golden brown.
When the dishes are cooked, turn the oven down to R$\frac{1}{4}$/90°C/ 200°F to keep them warm.

17 When the spinach is ready, drain off any water very well through a sieve or colander and put in a vegetable dish. If the pie is ready to serve, stand both the vegetable dish and pie on the mats on the table. If the pie is not quite ready, keep the spinach in a warm place.

A Quick Lunch to Prepare and Cook : Grilled Lamb Chops with Mint Sauce : Creamed Potatoes and Peas : Banana Custard

For 2

Food to collect for banana custard

2 bananas
2 teacups of milk
1 rounded tablespoon sugar
1 heaped tablespoon custard powder
1 small chocolate flake bar

Food to collect for lamb chops, potatoes and peas

2 lamb chops
a small jar of mint sauce
vinegar
1 packet dried potatoes to serve 2–3
1 small packet frozen peas
salt
a little butter, or margarine, or cooking oil

Equipment to collect

a chopping board
a vegetable knife
a measuring jug
a basin
a grill-pan
a 1 pt/½ l dish for the banana custard
a large serving plate for the meat
2 saucepans
a clean cloth to dry the chops
a meat skewer
a colander
1 tablespoon
1 wooden spoon
1 knife and fork for turning the meat

Preparation
* Wash your hands. Put on your apron.
* Collect the food and equipment. Put neatly on the work-top.
* Make sure there is an oven-cloth near the stove.

Method of work

Preparation of banana custard:

1 Rinse a milk saucepan with cold water, tip this away, then measure the milk into the pan. Leave the pan on the table for the moment.

2 Measure out the custard powder and sugar and put into a basin. Take 2 tablespoons of cold milk from the saucepan and put with the custard powder and sugar. Blend or mix together the milk and custard powder until you have a smooth liquid with NO lumps.

3 Put the milk on to boil and keep a careful watch on it. Remember that when nearing the boil, milk suddenly rises in the pan and will overflow.

4 So, once you see the tiny bubbles covering the surface of the milk, but before it rises, take off the heat and stand on a heat-proof mat on your work-top. Pour a little of the hot milk on the blended custard powder and stir well with a wooden spoon. Then tip it all back into the saucepan, stir again making sure there are no lumps. Then put back on to the heat, stirring all the time. When it boils again, turn down the heat to LOW or the lowest number marked and continue to stir until the custard is evenly thick – this will only take about 30 seconds. Put back on the heat-proof mat on your work-top.

5 Quickly unzip the bananas and with a vegetable knife cut them into rings on your chopping board. Put the bananas into the custard and pour into the dish. Give the dish a little shake to level off the custard.
If you cut the bananas some time before you need them for the custard they will turn brown in the air unless you squeeze lemon juice over them straight away.

6 Leave the banana custard to cool before decorating it.

7 PUT TO WARM
a serving plate for the meat   2 dinner plates

Set the table with:

2 place-mats or a cloth	2 dessert plates or dishes
2 paper serviettes	salt, pepper and mustard
2 dinner knives and forks	3 table-mats and 2 table or
2 dessert spoons	serving spoons

8 Put the grill on HIGH or the highest heat marked. Put the grill-pan and grid on the work-top.

9 From the bottle of mint, put some into a small jug or sauce boat. Add just a little vinegar to your own taste. Put the jug of mint sauce on the table with a spoon.

10 Wash the chops quickly and dry in a clean cloth.

11 Put on the grill grid and put a knob of margarine or butter on top of each chop. Or you can brush over each side of the chops with oil.

12 Put under the grill. The chops should take about 15 minutes to cook but, of course, it does depend on their thickness. You will have to turn them once so they get a rich brown on each side.

13 Read the instructions on the packet of peas. Measure out the water into a saucepan and put on to boil with a pinch of salt. You will be wise to turn on the BACK hotplate or to light the BACK gas ring so you have a cool place in the front of the stove to stand dishes or plates.

14 Read the instructions on the packet of potatoes. Measure out the water into a saucepan and put on to boil, again use the BACK heat.

15 Leave the chocolate flake in the wrapper and crush it finely. Then carefully open the wrapper and sprinkle the chocolate over the COLD banana custard. Put the dish on the table.

16 Put the peas into the water when it comes to the boil. Look at the clock to time them.

17 Look at the chops. Wait until the first side of both the fat and lean meat is really a deep brown before turning them over. Now you have three things to watch. If two things need attention at the same time, just remove one of them from the heat until you can deal with it. Remember that if no heat is passing to it, it will not spoil.

18 Turn the chops over when the first side is cooked, using a knife and fork. Put under the grill again.

19 When the water for the potatoes comes to the boil, take the saucepan off the stove and put on a heat-proof mat on the work-top. Add the packet of potatoes and stir well with a wooden spoon. Put in a knob of butter and continue stirring with a wooden spoon until thick and smooth. Fetch the serving plate you put to warm and pile the potatoes up in the middle. Put it back into a warm place.

20 When the peas are cooked, stand the colander in the sink and strain them. When the water has stopped dripping, get the serving plate again and arrange the peas either side of the potatoes. Put back into a warm place.

21 Look at the chops, if the second side is a deep brown, take the meat skewer and pierce the middle of the lean part. If red or pink juice appears, the chops need more cooking, if you see colourless juice or nothing at all then they are ready.

22 Put the serving dish on top of the stove and with a knife and fork, stand each chop against the pile of potatoes, next to the peas.

23 Turn off the stove and put the serving plate on a heat-proof mat on the table, together with the warm dinner plates.

Liver, Tomato and Bacon Casserole, Jacket Potatoes, Brussels Sprouts : Rice Pudding

For 2

Food to collect for casserole

2 slices of lambs liver
2 rashers of bacon
1 small tin of tomatoes
1 meat cube
a knob of butter or margarine
pepper and salt

Food to collect for the potatoes and brussels sprouts

2–4 medium sized potatoes
a knob of butter for each potato
1 small packet of frozen brussels sprouts

Food to collect for the rice pudding

2 level tablespoons of pudding rice
1 tablespoon of sugar
2 teacupsful of milk
a pinch of nutmeg

Equipment to collect

a deep heatproof (1 pt/$\frac{1}{2}$ l) dish for rice
a casserole dish for liver
a chopping board
a tin-opener
a meat skewer
a colander
a baking tray
a saucepan for the sprouts
1 tablespoon
1 vegetable knife
a sieve
a kettle

Preparation

* Wash your hands. Put on your apron.

* Collect the food and equipment. Put neatly on the work-top.
* Put the oven on at R2/150°C/300°F. Put a shelf at the top of the oven for the liver casserole. Put a shelf in the middle of the oven for the rice and a shelf at the bottom of the oven for the jacket potatoes. Make sure there is an oven-cloth nearby.

Method of work

For this meal we must think carefully about the order in which we prepare the dishes and put them in the oven to cook.

The rice pudding takes about $1\frac{1}{2}$ hours at R2/150°C/300°F.

The jacket potatoes take about $1\frac{1}{4}$ hours at the same temperature.

The casserole takes about 45 minutes at the same temperature.

The brussels sprouts need 8–10 minutes of simmering.

To get everything cooked and ready to serve at the same time you must first decide at what time you want your lunch, then work out on paper at what time each dish should be prepared and cooked so that it is ready by lunchtime.

For a lunch at 12.00, your timetable should look like this:

Time	Order of work
10.00	Wash your hands. Put on your apron. Collect the food and equipment. Put neatly on the work-top. Put the oven on at R2/150°C/300°F. Check the oven shelves.
10.15	Prepare the rice.

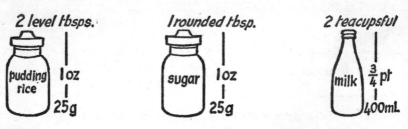

2 level tbsps. — pudding rice — 1 oz — 25g

1 rounded tbsp. — sugar — 1 oz — 25g

2 teacupsful — milk — $\frac{3}{4}$ pt — 400mL

10.30 Put the rice into the oven.
       Wipe over the work-top.
10.40 Scrub and prepare the potatoes.
10.45 Put them into the oven.
       Wash up, wipe up and put away.
10.50 Prepare the liver casserole.
11.15 Put it into the oven.
       Wipe over the work-top. Wash up, wipe up and put away.
11.25 Put plates and dishes to warm.
11.30 Set the table.
11.45 Put water on to boil for brussels sprouts.
11.50 Put brussels sprouts on to cook.
       Dish food, if ready.
12.00 Serve food at the table.

Preparing the rice

1 Measure out the rice and sugar. Put the rice in a sieve and rinse
  under the cold water tap. Shake off any drops of water and
  put in the deep, heat-proof dish. Sprinkle over the sugar and
  pour in the milk. Stand the dish on a baking tray and put on
  to the middle shelf of the oven. It will take about $1\frac{1}{2}$ hours to
  cook.

2 Pick out the potatoes as near the same size as possible. If
  they have been cleaned already just wash them in warm water.
  If they still have a coating of earth they will need to be scrub-
  bed clean in a bowl of hot water. Remember to rinse the
  brush, bowl and sink afterwards.

3 Put the potatoes on your chopping board and with the tip of
  a vegetable knife cut round the middle of each potato just
  breaking the skin. This is called scoring the potato and is done
  for the same reason as cutting round the middle of the apple,
  see diagram on page 52, or pricking the sausages. Can you
  remember the reason?
  Place the potatoes on a metal plate or a baking tray and put

on the bottom shelf of the oven. They will take about $1\frac{1}{4}$ hours to cook.

4 Wipe over the work-top. Stack the used equipment by the sink, then wash and wipe up.

Preparing the liver casserole:

5 First open the tin of tomatoes carefully or get someone to open them for you.

Grease the bottom part of the casserole dish with a knob of butter or margarine.

Put the meat cube into a basin or a measure and add two tablespoons of HOT water to dissolve it. Stir with a spoon until there are no lumps left. Then tip in the tin of tomatoes and mix together.

6 Look at the liver; if you can see any tubes in the slices cut them out with either kitchen scissors or with a vegetable knife on a chopping board. Wash the liver and leave it wet and put into the casserole dish. Add a pinch of salt and pepper. If the rashers of bacon have a rind on them cut it off. Put the bacon on top of the liver in the casserole dish. Pour over the meat juice and tomatoes. Cover with the lid of the dish and put on the baking tray. This must be put in the oven 45 minutes before it is due to be served. It needs to go on the top shelf.

At this time take out the rice and stand it on top of the stove. If it has a skin on top which looks a dark colour then you can stir it to the bottom of the dish or take it off altogether. This is the time to sprinkle a little nutmeg over the top if you like it. Put the rice back into the oven and close the door.

7 Wipe over the work-top. Stack the used equipment then wash and wipe up. Any equipment or food that you will not use again can be put away.

Put to warm	Set the table with:
2 dinner plates	2 place-mats or a cloth
2 dessert plates	2 paper serviettes
1 vegetable dish for the brussels sprouts	4 serving or tablespoons
	3 heat-proof mats
1 plate or dish for the jacket potatoes	2 dinner knives and forks
	2 dessert spoons

8 Just 15 minutes before you want to serve lunch, read the instructions on the packet of brussels sprouts. Measure out the water into a saucepan and put on to boil. You would be wise to use a BACK gas ring or hot plate so that you can use the front part to stand dishes or plates on as you get them from the oven.

Add a pinch of salt to the water and put in the brussels sprouts when the water boils. Bring back to the boil then look at the clock to time them for about 8 minutes. Put the heat on MEDIUM so that they simmer.

9 While the brussels sprouts are simmering, get each dish out of the oven and put on top of the stove to test.

First the liver casserole should be nice and moist. Take a meat skewer and put it through a slice of liver. If red or pink juice appears, then the liver needs more cooking but make sure it is from the liver and not the tomatoes. If you see colourless juice or none at all, then it is ready, so keep it in a warm place. Take out the potatoes and put safely on top of the stove. Hold one of the potatoes in the oven-cloth and give it a good squeeze to see if it is soft inside. If so, put them in the dish you have put to warm with their splits showing. Then you can put a knob of butter in each potato by opening the split middle a little more. Keep in a warm place.

10 Now take out the rice and with a spoon scoop up a little from the corner. It should be nice and creamy with not too much milk because during the cooking it should have gone inside the grains of rice, making them large and soft. If you are in any doubt, you can taste a little on the spoon. Remember to wash the spoon before using it again. If it is cooked, put it in a warm place. If not, it can continue to cook while you are eating the casserole.

11 If one or two of the dishes need further cooking, leave the oven on. If they are all cooked, then turn it down to R$\frac{1}{4}$/90°C/200°F and leave the door ajar. You will then have a large space for keeping all the dishes warm.

12 Lastly, if you have timed the brussels sprouts you can check whether they are cooked by putting a meat skewer into one of them. If cooked, it should be soft. Stand the colander in the sink and strain them. When the water has stopped dripping get the vegetable dish you warmed and put them in.

Once again if all the dishes for the main course are cooked you can serve them on the table. If you are waiting for any to finish cooking, then keep the brussels sprouts warm. To stop them from drying up, put a knob of butter on the top.

Afternoon Teas

Again, this is another time during the day when a refreshment is very acceptable. If you are at home it is usually eaten from a tray or a small table or a trolley, say in the sitting-room. Small, dainty portions of food are served such as biscuits, sandwiches, scones or cakes. Therefore only tea plates and paper serviettes are needed. More information about the making of tea is given on page 23.

Sandwiches

Food to Collect for Sandwiches

1 thin sliced loaf
butter

Ideas for savoury sandwiches

1 Cold meat; for example, ham, tongue, spam with pickle.
2 Fish; for example, salmon, tuna, sardine with cucumber.
3 Egg; for example, chopped hard-boiled egg with mustard and cress and sandwich spread.
4 Cheese, grated with a little sandwich spread.
5 Paste.

Equipment to collect

a bread board
an ordinary knife
a bread knife
a bread plate
basin to put fillings in when made

Ideas for sweet sandwiches

6 Mashed banana and lemon.

7 Honey.

8 Peanut butter.

9 Chocolate spread.

To make really nice sandwiches, you need fresh bread, and a good tasting filling that once put between the bread will stay there and not fall out. Therefore try to make the filling into the form of a paste that can be spread. Most slices of food, for example, cheese, meat or cucumber are quite all right to use.

Preparation

* Wash your hands. Put on your apron.

* Collect the food and equipment. Put neatly on the work-top.

Method of work

Preparing the fillings:

1 *Meat*: slices of meat will have to be trimmed to fit the size of the slice of bread, but you can do this as you are making the sandwiches. Put a little pickle on a plate.

2 *Fish:* open the tin carefully and pour off the liquid or oil. Empty the contents into a basin and mash it up with a fork. Mix in just a teaspoon of vinegar. Wipe the cucumber, then, with a vegetable knife slice it as thinly as possible. When you are ready to fill the sandwiches put the fish filling on first, then cover with about four slices of cucumber, and the other slice of bread.

3 *Cheese:* grate some hard cheese on to a plate. Mix with it about one teaspoon of sandwich spread to make it into a paste. If you want to use sliced cheese, then put the sandwich spread on to the buttered side of the bread first, then put the slice of cheese on top and lastly the second piece of bread.

4 *Egg:* in order to chop the egg, it must be hard-boiled. Half-fill

66

a saucepan with water and put on to boil. The heat should be at HIGH or the highest number marked. When big bubbles are moving about in the water, carefully lower the egg to the bottom of a saucepan on a tablespoon. Look at the time, the egg will take 10 minutes once the water begins to boil again. Prepare the cress, by cutting off the punnet where it has been growing and putting it in a colander. Wash it under the tap, wait until the water has stopped dripping, then spread out on a clean tea towel to dry.

When the egg has been boiling for 10 minutes, turn off the heat. Carefully carry the saucepan to the sink, lift out the egg with a tablespoon and put in a basin of cold water.

Leave until the egg is cool enough to shell. If you do not put the egg into cold water straight away a black mark develops around the outside of the yolk as it cools. This is due to iron sulphide forming. Once cool, crack the shell and put the bits into a piece of old newspaper. If the shell is difficult to remove, try taking it off under running water. But pick up all the bits of shell afterwards.

With a cook's knife chop up the egg on a chopping board, as small as you can, then put into a basin. Mix it with a teaspoon of sandwich spread or salad cream and add a pinch of salt.

When using the filling, spread the egg mixture on to the first slice of buttered bread. Then sprinkle over the cress. Then firmly press down the second slice of buttered bread.

Sweet fillings: unzip the bananas and put on to a plate. Mash them well with a fork. Add about a teaspoon of lemon juice to stop them going brown. All the other fillings are in a paste form, but a small quantity should be put out on to a plate and used from that. Do not dip into the jar for every slice of bread you fill or you will get butter in the jar.

Preparing the sandwiches:

6 To make sure that the sandwiches fit together when paired up, take two slices of bread from the packet at a time. Spread butter on the two insides, the sides that were touching. Take the butter to the very edge of the slice.

7 With a clean knife, spread the filling on to just one slice. Then on to the filling, fit the second buttered slice of bread.

8 With a flat hand press down to make it firm.

9 Put this sandwich aside and pick up two more slices of bread, remember which two sides you are going to butter.

10 When you have made enough sandwiches, put the pile you have made on the bread board and cut into quarters with the bread knife.

11 Arrange neatly on the plate. Savoury sandwiches look more attractive on a dish paper. Sweet sandwiches look daintier on a paper doily.

Rock Cakes

These are to look, but not taste, like rocks!

Makes 8

Food to collect
4 heaped tablespoons of self-raising flour (see page 9)

Equipment to collect
a mixing bowl
a sieve

4 level tablespoons granulated
    sugar (see page 9)
2 equal portions margarine
    (see page 9)
1 small egg
2 rounded tablespoons of
    currants or sultanas
    (see page 9)
a little lard or cooking oil

a basin
a plate
a baking tray
2 ordinary knives
1 fork
1 tablespoon
1 palette knife
newspaper
an egg whisk
a cooling tray

Preparation

* Wash your hands. Put on your apron.
* Collect the food and equipment. Put neatly on the work-top.
* Put the oven on at R8/235°C/450°F. Put a shelf at the top of the oven. Make sure there is an oven-cloth nearby.
* Spread half a sheet of newspaper on the work-top. Measure out the currants or sultanas, put in a sieve and rest on the newspaper. Spoon on to the dried fruit one tablespoon of flour. Hold the sieve in one hand and stir round with a spoon held in the other. Of course, all the flour will fall out on to the paper, but so will any bits and pieces from the fruit and you will be left with them cleaned. Put the fruit on a plate. Bang the sieve on to the sides of the sink to clean it, but do not wet it, otherwise the mixture of flour and water will be difficult to remove.
* Rub a little lard, or brush a little oil, over the baking tray.

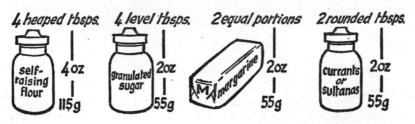

4 heaped tbsps. self-raising flour — 4 oz / 115g
4 level tbsps. granulated sugar — 2 oz / 55g
2 equal portions margarine — 2 oz / 55g
2 rounded tbsps. currants or sultanas — 2 oz / 55g

Method of work

1 Measure out the flour, sieve it into the mixing bowl.

   Measure out the sugar and put on to the plate with the cleaned fruit.

   Measure out the margarine and put into the mixing bowl with the flour. Crack a small egg on the side of the basin, hold it over the basin with two hands and open out the shell where it is cracked.

   Put the empty shell in the newspaper. With either an egg whisk or a fork, beat the egg until both the yolk and the white are thoroughly mixed together.

2 With an ordinary knife cut up the margarine in the flour. Then rub in with your fingers until it looks like fine bread-crumbs.

3 Mix in the sugar and dried fruit. Stir round with your fork.

4 Make a well in the centre, ready to put in the egg. When mixed and ready for cooking this mixture has got to be quite stiff so that it remains in the shape of rocks. If it is too sticky once in the oven, the heat will melt the margarine and dissolve the sugar so that the mixture will spread over the baking tray. Therefore add the egg a little at a time until you can bind the mixture together, but it is still stiff enough to stand your fork upright.

5 With the fork and a knife divide the mixture into 8 equal pieces and place them on the baking tray 2 in/5 cm apart. The base

of the mixture should be the biggest part, narrowing off to a point at the top to look like rocks.

6 Put the baking tray on the top shelf of the oven. Look at the time. They will only take about 10–12 minutes.

7 This will give you time to wipe over the work-top. Stack the used equipment beside the sink. Then put out a cooling tray or the grid from the grill-pan.

8 After 10 minutes open the door and look at the cakes:
    they should smell good
    they should have risen because you used self-raising flour
    they should look golden brown and quite dry
    they should feel firm to the touch and not leave a finger mark.

9 If the rock cakes pass those tests, then leave them on the top of the stove to cool a little. Turn off the oven. When the tray has cooled, put the cooling tray next to the baking tray and take each one off on a palette knife.

Jam Tarts

Makes 10

Food to collect

$\frac{1}{2}$ small packet of frozen, shortcrust pastry
about 3 tablespoons of jam
a little lard or cooking oil

Equipment to collect

a bun tin
a cutter $\frac{1}{4}$ in/1 cm larger than the holes in the tin
a rolling pin
a flour dredger filled with plain flour
a cook's knife
a palette knife
a plate for jam
a cooking tray

Preparation

* The pastry must be at room temperature for $1-1\frac{1}{2}$ hours before using it.
* Wash your hands. Put on your apron.
* Collect the food and equipment. Put neatly on the work-top.
* Put the oven on at R6/205°C/400°F. Make sure there is a shelf one-third from the top of the oven. Make sure there is an oven-cloth nearby.
* Rub a little lard or brush a little oil in the holes of the bun tin.
* Put the jam out on to a plate.

Method of work

1 Lightly sprinkle flour on the work-top to stop the pastry from sticking to it. Flour one part of the rolling pin and brush it all round with your hand.
2 Put the pastry on the floured work-top. Loosely hold the rolling pin at each end between your thumb and fingers.
3 Put the rolling pin down lightly on to the edge of the pastry and let it roll the length of your hands. Then pick it up.
4 Next put the rolling pin down where you left off last time. Roll the pastry and again pick up the pin. Do not bang down the pin or steam roller the pastry, otherwise it will not be light to eat.
5 When you have worked your way up the pastry so all of it has been rolled once, pick up the pastry over the rolling pin and look to see if the work-top needs another dusting of flour. It is better to sprinkle a little flour often than a lot all at once.

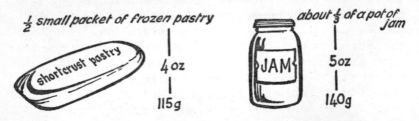

$\frac{1}{2}$ small packet of frozen pastry

shortcrust pastry

4 oz

115g

about $\frac{1}{3}$ of a pot of jam

JAM

5 oz

140g

6 Put the pastry down the same way as before and roll it over again.

7 Pick the pastry up over the rolling pin again and this time turn the pastry round. Roll it twice that way.

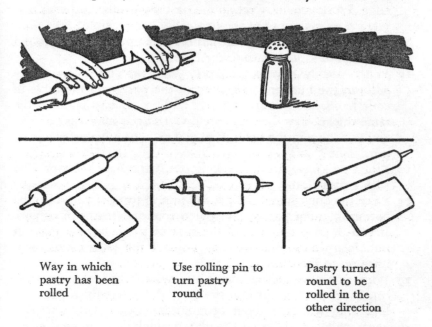

Way in which pastry has been rolled

Use rolling pin to turn pastry round

Pastry turned round to be rolled in the other direction

Make sure you roll the pastry evenly. It should look smooth and the same thickness. Never turn the pastry over, only roll on the same side. This is called the 'best' side.

8 Continue to roll the pastry, first one way and then the other, so that the pastry grows in both directions.

9 Because the jam tarts are going to be cut out with the cutter, you do not have to worry too much about the shape of it, only about the thickness. For tartlet cases the pastry needs to be one tenth of an inch or one fifth of a centimetre which is quite thin, but the pastry will swell a little in the oven.

10 When you have finished rolling the pastry, put down the rolling pin, take the cutter and starting from one edge cut as close to it as you can. Leave the cut out pastry on the table. Cut out the next one, close to the first and still keeping on the edge. Work your way round the pastry with the cutter so that you get as many out of the first rolling as possible.

11 Put your bun tin next to the pastry, pick up each pastry round and carefully fit them into the holes.

12 You probably have some pastry left over and a few empty holes in the bun tin. So collect all the pastry on the table in your hand, then flour the table and roll it out again to the same thickness as the first batch. Cut out as many as you can and put them in the holes. Can you roll out any pastry for the third time?

13 When you have finished rolling out, wipe over the work-top with a dish-cloth.

14 Place the bun tin and the plate of jam in front of you. Into the bottom of each pastry case put a rounded teaspoon of jam. If you put too much jam, the heat of the oven will make it bubble up and spill over the sides of the pastry making it burn on to the tin.

15 When you have finished, wipe off any crumbs or jam from the tin. Then put the tin into the oven about one-third from the top. They will take about 15 minutes.

16 Meanwhile, wipe over the work-top, stack the used equipment by the sink and put away the ingredients. Get out a cooling tray or grill grid.

17 When cooked the pastry should look a pale biscuit colour and quite dry. It will have shrunk away from the sides slightly.

18 If cooked, put the bun tin on top of the stove until it has cooled down a little. Then place it on the work-top beside the cooling tray. With a palette knife gently raise one side of each jam tart. Pick up with the other hand and place it on the cooling tray.

Plain Scones

**For plain scones follow the same recipe and method as
for cheese scones on page 42**

Of course, you leave out the cheese, so you will not need to
collect a cheese-grater as part of the equipment. But you need 1
level tablespoon sugar. In the **Method of work** miss out number
3, but add your sugar instead. Serve the scones cut in half and
spread with butter and jam. They are also nice served toasted
and hot and spread with butter.

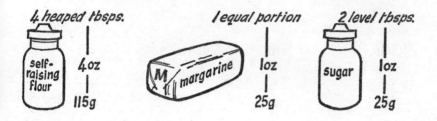

4 heaped tbsps.   self-raising flour   4oz   115g

1 equal portion   margarine   1oz   25g

2 level tbsps.   sugar   1oz   25g

High Teas or Suppers

If the main meal of the day is taken at lunchtime, then the next meal you are likely to have is a high tea or a supper. This can include a light meal of meat, fish, cheese or eggs followed by bread, butter, jam and cakes with tea or milk.

Just as breakfast, and lunch or dinner, this is eaten at the table. If young children go to bed after this meal then they should not eat too much or eat anything that is too rich otherwise they will not have a very peaceful night.

Welsh Rarebit : Bread and Butter and Jam : Cakes : Tea

For 2

Food to collect

8 tablespoons of grated cheese
a pinch of dry mustard
a pinch of salt
4 tablespoons of milk
2 tomatoes
a sprig of parsley, if possible
2 thick slices of bread for toast
butter for spreading on toast and bread

4 thin slices of bread
jam
cakes

Equipment to collect

a plate
a cheese-grater
a bread board
a chopping board
an ordinary knife
a large plate for bread and butter
a plate for cakes
a kettle

Preparation

* Wash your hands. Put on your apron.
* Collect the food and equipment. Put neatly on the work-top.
* Put the jam into a dish.
* Hold the stalks of parsley and rinse the sprigs under water. Shake them well, then break off all the stalks so only the sprigs are left.
* Grate the cheese on to a plate, using the smallest holes on the grater.
* Set the table.

For the Table

2 place-mats or a cloth
2 table-mats
2 paper serviettes
2 dinner knives and forks
2 dessert knives
2 tea plates
2 teacups, saucers and spoons
a sugar bowl and spoon

a milk jug
a jam dish and spoon
salt and pepper
a teapot stand and teapot

PUT TO WARM
2 dessert plates

Method of work

1 Take the thin slices of bread and butter them on the bread board with an ordinary knife. Arrange on the plate.
2 Set a doily on another plate and put out some cakes. Put both bread and cakes on the table.
3 Fill the kettle and put on to boil. If it boils before you are ready to use the water, turn it off or take off the heat. Then reboil it when you need it.
4 Put on the grill to heat for the toast.

Preparing the welsh rarebit:

5 To the grated cheese add a pinch of mustard and salt and the milk. With a fork, mix the milk in well until it becomes smooth.

6 Put the toast under the grill. Warm the teapot.

7 With a vegetable knife, cut the tomatoes in half on the chopping board, see page 30.

8 When the toast is a golden brown on the first side turn it over and put the halves of tomatoes under the grill as well.

9 The second side of the toast must only be a light brown so stand near the grill ready to take it off.

10 When the toast is just beginning to colour, turn the grill down to MEDIUM, take the toast off but leave the tomatoes under. Put the toast on the bread board and butter the lightest sides. Then spread the cheese mixture on each slice of toast. Take back to the grill on a plate and put back under the heat until the cheese melts and turns a golden brown colour.

11 Meanwhile, empty the hot water from the teapot and put in the tea. Make sure the kettle is really boiling, then make the tea.

Put a cosy on the pot and place on the teapot stand on the table.

12 See if the welsh rarebit is ready. If so, put on the warm plates, sit a sprig of parsley in the middle of each piece of toast and the tomatoes either side of the toast.

Put the plates on the table.

Scrambled Egg on Toast : Bread and Butter and Jam : Cakes : Tea

For 2

Food to collect
2 large eggs
a knob of margarine
2 tablespoons of milk
pepper and salt

Equipment to collect
a thick-based saucepan
a basin
an egg whisk or a fork
a bread board

78

2 thick slices of bread for
  toast
butter for toast and bread
4 thin slices of bread
jam
cakes

a plate for cakes
1 tablespoon
1 ordinary knife
a kettle
a wooden spoon

Preparation

* Wash your hands. Put on your apron.
* Collect the food and equipment. Put neatly on the work-top.
* Put the jam into a dish.
* Set the table.

For the table

2 place-mats or a cloth
2 table-mats
2 paper serviettes
2 dinner knives and forks
2 dessert knives
2 tea plates
2 teacups, saucers and spoons
a sugar bowl and spoon

a milk jug
a jam dish and spoon
salt and pepper
a teapot stand and teapot

PUT TO WARM
2 dessert plates

Method of work

1 Take the thin slices of bread and butter them on the bread
  board with an ordinary knife. Remember to cover the whole
  slice with butter. Arrange on the plate.
2 Set a doily on another plate and put out some cakes. Put both
  the bread and the cakes on the table.
3 Fill the kettle and put on to boil. If it boils before you are ready
  to use the water, turn it off or take off the heat. Then reboil
  it when you need it.
4 Put on the grill to heat for the toast.

Preparing scrambled egg:

5 Tap the eggs on the side of the basin to crack the shell, hold
the egg over the basin and pull apart at the crack. Let all the
yolk and white fall into the basin. Break the second egg the
same way. Beat the eggs together until the yolks and whites
are thoroughly mixed. Then add 2 tablespoons of milk to the
eggs and a pinch of pepper and salt.

6 Put a knob of margarine into the pan and put on to the heat at
LOW or on the lowest number.

7 Put the toast under the grill. Warm the teapot.

8 When the margarine has melted, take the eggs and a wooden
spoon to the stove, pour the eggs into the pan and allow to
set at the bottom of the pan. This will take a few seconds. Then
stir the set egg with a spoon and the remaining liquid will take
its place.

9 Are you keeping an eye on the toast? When it is a golden
brown on the first side, turn it over.

10 As soon as all the egg has nicely 'set' or scrambled, turn off
the heat but leave on the stove until the toast is ready.

11 Tip away the hot water from the teapot, make sure the water
is really boiling, put the tea in the pot and make the tea. Put
a cosy on the pot and stand on the table.

12 When the toast is ready, turn off the grill. Take the toast to
the bread board and butter it. Put it on the warm plates.
With a tablespoon put the scrambled eggs on the toast.

Put the plates on the table.

Cheese and Ham Dreams : Soft Rolls and Jam : Scones and Cakes : Tea

For 2

Food to Collect	**Equipment to collect**
2 slices of ham	a bread board

2 slices of cheese to fit a
   slice of bread
4 thin slices of bread
butter

2 soft rolls
jam
cakes or scones

a plate for rolls and butter
a plate for cakes
1 vegetable knife
1 ordinary knife
a chopping board

Preparation

* Wash your hands. Put on your apron.
* Collect the food and equipment. Put neatly on the work-top.
* Put the jam into the dish.
* The pre-packed slices of cheese are suitable for this. If you are cutting your own slices off a large piece of cheese, stand it on the board and cut down. It may tend to break, but all the cheese can be used no matter how small the pieces.
* Set the table.

For the table

2 place-mats or a cloth
2 table-mats
2 paper serviettes
2 dinner knives and forks
2 dessert knives
2 tea plates
2 teacups, saucers and spoons
a sugar bowl and spoon

a milk jug
a jam dish and spoon
salt and pepper
a dish of chutney, if liked
a teapot stand and teapot

PUT TO WARM
2 dessert plates

Method of work

1 Cut the soft rolls in half and butter them. Put on the plate.
2 Set a doily on another plate and put out some cakes.
3 Put both the rolls and cakes on the table.

Fill the kettle and put it on to boil. Put on the grill to heat for the toast.

Preparing the cheese and ham dreams:

4 Take the slices of bread and butter them on a bread board with an ordinary knife.

5 Now as if you were making sandwiches, place the ham on two of the buttered slices. On top of the ham put the slices of cheese. Then place the other slices of bread on the cheese, buttered sides down. With the flat of your hand press the sandwiches down firmly.

6 With a bread knife trim off the crusts around the sandwiches. Then cut in halves and place on the grill grid with a knob of butter on each half. Put under the heat and toast to a golden brown on both sides.

7 Pour some hot water from the kettle to warm the teapot. If the kettle boils and you are not ready to use it, turn it off or take it off the heat. Then reboil it when you need it.
While you are waiting for the toast to brown, wipe over the work-top, stack any used dishes and put away any food no longer wanted.

8 When the first sides are a golden brown, turn the dreams over. Put another knob of butter on each half and put under the heat.

9 Empty the hot water from the teapot, put in the tea, make sure the kettle is boiling then make the tea. Put a cosy on the teapot and place on the teapot stand on the table.

10 Look at the cheese and ham dreams. They should be nicely browned with the cheese melting from the middle.
Place two halves on each plate and serve at the table.
Did you remember to turn off the grill?

Fish Fingers : Mashed Potatoes : Grilled Tomatoes : Bread, Butter and Jam : Cakes : Tea

For 2

Food to collect

1 small packet of frozen fish fingers
1 packet of dried potatoes to serve 2–3
2 tomatoes
1 slice of lemon
2 sprigs of parsley, if possible

4 thin slices of bread
butter
jam
cakes

Equipment to collect

a saucepan
a large plate for bread and butter
a plate for cakes
a bread board
1 tablespoon
1 ordinary knife
a chopping board
a wooden spoon
a kettle

Preparation

* Wash your hands. Put on your apron.
* Collect the food and equipment. Put neatly on the work-top.
* Hold the stalks of parsley and rinse the sprigs under water. Shake well, then break off all the stalks so only the sprigs are left.
* Cut the lemon slice into butterfly decorations, as shown on page 85.
* Put the jam into a dish.
* Set the table.

For the table

2 place-mats or a cloth	a milk jug
2 table-mats	a jam dish and spoon
2 paper serviettes	salt and pepper
2 fish knives and forks	a teapot stand and teapot
2 dessert knives	
2 tea plates	
2 teacups, saucers and spoons	PUT TO WARM
a sugar bowl and spoon	2 dessert plates

Method of work

1 Take the thin slices of bread and butter them on the bread board with an ordinary knife. Arrange on a plate.

2 Set a doily on another plate and put out some cakes. Put both the bread and cakes on the table.

3 Fill the kettle and put on to boil. If it boils before you are ready to use the water, turn it off or take it off the heat. Then reboil it when you need it.

Preparing the fish fingers, potatoes and tomatoes:

4 Put on the grill to heat for the fish fingers and tomatoes.

5 Read the instructions on the packet of potatoes. Measure out the water you need and put on to boil. Put on a BACK gas ring or hot plate so you can stand dishes on the front.

6 Read the instructions on the packet of fish fingers. Notice how long they need to cook for, then put them on the grill-pan. Dot each fish finger with a little margarine or butter. Put under the heat and look at the time.

7 Warm the teapot.

8 With a vegetable knife, cut the tomatoes in halves on the chopping board.

9 As soon as the fish fingers are a golden brown on one side, turn them over. Then put the tomatoes under the grill.

10 When the water is boiling for the potatoes take it off the

84

heat and put it on a heat-proof mat on the work-top. Turn off the gas ring or hot plate. Add the packet of potatoes and stir well with a wooden spoon. When they are thick and smooth, put in a knob of butter and stir it in. Then put back on the stove to keep warm.

11 Look at the fish fingers and tomatoes, if they are browning too quickly lower the heat.

12 Empty the hot water from the teapot. Then put in the tea. Make sure the kettle is boiling, then make the tea. Put a cosy on the pot and place on the stand on the table.

13 As soon as the fish fingers are browned both sides, look at the time to see if they have had long enough cooking.
Set the warmed plates on the work-top so that when the fish fingers are ready you can serve out all the hot food. Put a lemon butterfly on the fish fingers. Place the plates on the table.

14 Turn off the grill heat and put the saucepan to soak in warm water.

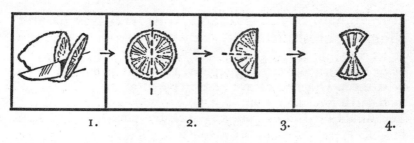

1.   2.   3.   4.

Cut a slice from a lemon (1) and cut the slice into half (2). Cut each half slice almost to the white centre (3) and then gently open it out (4).

Packed Meals

If you are planning an outing or even taking a packed lunch to school every day, do start to get it ready the day or night before. In a packed meal you want a variety of foods that can be packed and carried without spoilage. You have to think of the containers or wrappers you need for packing. Polythene, tinfoil and grease-proof paper are all good materials for keeping food fresh. Some foods need a rigid container, others will travel and arrive well in just a wrapper.

If you want to keep anything either very hot or very cold then you should use a thermos flask. If you have to carry the food a long way keep everything as light as possible. When you have wrapped all the foods carefully, remember to pack them tightly in a bag or basket with a flat bottom, to stop things from tilting.

Hot Tomato Soup : Sausage Rolls with Egg Salad : Mousse : Fresh Fruit

Some of these foods can be prepared the night or day before you need them. Other foods are best prepared at the latest possible moment before setting out.

You would need to prepare and cook the sausage rolls the day before.

You would also be wise to wash the salad ingredients the night before and store in a polythene bag in the refrigerator.

On the other hand, you would need to make the soup just before starting out so it has every chance of keeping hot in the thermos flask.

The other items can be fitted in depending how much time you have either the day before or the actual day that you need the packed meal.

Preparing the sausage rolls:

For 2

Food to collect	**Equipment to collect**
½ small packet of frozen shortcrust pastry	a pastry brush
	a basin
4 sausages	a saucer for the glaze
a little lard or cooking oil	a rolling pin
	a flour dredger filled with plain flour
	a cook's knife
	a baking tray
	a vegetable knife or kitchen scissors

Preparation

* The pastry must be at room temperature for 1–1½ hours before using it.
* Wash your hands. Put on your apron.
* Collect the food and equipment. Put neatly on the work-top.
* Put the oven on at R6/205°C/400°F. Make sure there is a shelf one-third from the top of the oven. Make sure there is an oven-cloth nearby.
* Rub a little lard or brush a little oil over the baking tray.
* Put some cold water in the basin for damping the pastry to make it stick together and put a tablespoon of milk in the saucer for the glaze.

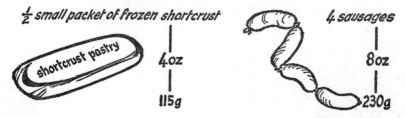

½ small packet of frozen shortcrust

shortcrust pastry

4oz

115g

4 sausages

8oz

230g

Method of work

1 All the instructions given for rolling out the pastry for jam tarts on page 72, must be remembered again.

2 For the sausage rolls, you want to roll the pastry into a square shape 8 in/20 cm. Therefore from the beginning you must start off with a square. If you use $\frac{1}{2}$ a small packet of frozen shortcrust pastry you will be starting off with a square.

3 In order to keep the square shape, first roll one way and then turn the pastry round and roll again, so that the square is growing in both directions. This is all you have to do until the pastry square is the size you need. If, however, the sides do get out of line, put down the rolling pin and use your hands to get it back into shape. Sometimes the corners of the square disappear; if this happens gently pull them out with your hands.

4 When rolled to the size, use the cook's knife to mark down the middle from left to right as shown. When you are sure you have two pastry strips of equal size, cut the pastry by just pressing on the knife.

Preparing the sausages:

5 With a vegetable knife or a pair of kitchen scissors, cut the sausage skin and peel it off. Put in newspaper to throw away. Flour the sausages slightly to stop them sticking. Join two sausages together by putting end to end. Then roll them to the length of the pastry strips. Now join the other two sausages together and roll them to the same length. Put each length of sausage on a pastry strip.

6 Dip the pastry brush into the water and damp along the four long edges of the pastry.

7 Pick up the long side of the pastry nearest you and as tightly as you can, roll it round the sausage meat until it overlaps the other edge of pastry. Press the edges firmly together with your fingers and then make sure the join is underneath.

8 in/20 cm

cut   8 in/20 cm

cut from left to right | damp the long edges | join underneath | three marks on the top

8 Now roll the other strip of pastry around the sausage in the same way.

9 Dip the pastry brush into the milk and glaze or brush along the top of both pastry rolls. This glaze will help to make the pastry a more attractive colour.

10 Mark each pastry roll in half. Then cut them in half, so you have four sausage rolls. On the top of each sausage roll, make three little snips with a pair of kitchen scissors or three small cuts with a knife. This is only a pattern, so just break the pastry to make it look attractive.

11 Put on a baking tray and cook on the shelf one-third from the top for 25–30 minutes. When cooked, they should smell good, the pastry should look a golden brown and the sausage meat should be browned. It is important that the meat is cooked through and not still red and raw.

Preparing the egg salad:

Food to collect
about $\frac{1}{4}$ of a lettuce
2 eggs
salad cream or mayonnaise
2 tomatoes
$\frac{1}{4}$ cucumber
salt

Equipment to collect

for lettuce:
    a bowl of water
    old newspaper
for eggs:
    a saucepan
    a basin
    a tablespoon

for tomatoes and cucumber
    a chopping board
    a vegetable knife
1 firm polythene container for
    the salad

1 Lettuce:
All the instructions given for preparing lettuce on page 47, nos 1–3, must be remembered again.

2 Tomatoes:
You can leave them whole, since they will travel better. They do need to be washed and wiped first.

3 Cucumber:
Wipe over the outside skin, then, with a vegetable knife, slice the cucumber down on the chopping board. The slices should be as thin as possible.

4 Hard-boiled eggs:
Do you remember how to hard-boil the eggs? If not, look on page 28, No 5.
When the eggs are hard-boiled and quite cold, put them on the chopping board and cut them in half lengthways.

Packing the egg salad:

First put the dry lettuce in a rigid container. Stand each half of the eggs, cut-side down, on the leaves of lettuce. Spoon over each half of egg just enough salad cream to coat.
Arrange the cucumber and tomatoes around the eggs.
A pinch of salt can be sprinkled over if you like.
Put the lid on tightly and if it is to be stored overnight, keep in the refrigerator.

Fresh fruit:
Apples and oranges are probably the best choice of fruit to take. Both will pack and carry well. Both will quench your thirst if you become dry.

Mousse:
These only need to be taken from the ice-box to be packed in the bag at the last minute.

Preparing the hot tomato soup:

Food to collect	Equipment to collect
1 packet of soup	a thermos flask
	a saucepan
	a wooden spoon
	a measure

1 Really, the amount of soup you make depends on how much your thermos-flask will hold. You can always check up by filling the thermos-flask with water then tipping the water into a measuring jug.

2 Now find out how much the packet of soup makes.
If you decide to make half the quantity, remember to halve both the soup powder and the water.

3 Make sure that the thermos-flask, cups and top are perfectly clean. At the same time test that the flask does not leak, by filling it with water and fitting on the cups and top. Dry the outside very well, then carefully hold the flask upside-down. If water appears you know that either the top is not on properly or else the flask is not sound.

4 Read the instructions on the packet of soup. Put the soup powder in the saucepan. Measure out the water and slowly stir it into the saucepan with a wooden spoon. Put the heat on HIGH or the highest heat marked to bring to the boil. You will be wise to stand by the soup to stir it with a wooden spoon every now and again. When you see big bubbles covering the surface turn the heat down to a medium heat, so that the soup

just simmers. It will need to simmer for about 4 minutes. Look at the clock.

5 Meanwhile pour hot water into the flask and let it stand to warm through.

6 When the soup is ready, turn off the stove and stand the pan on a heat-proof mat on your work-top. Empty out the water from the flask. Then using a cup or a measure, take the soup from the saucepan to the thermos-flask. When filled, put the top on straight away and make sure it is tightly fitted. Wipe the outside over with a dish-cloth.

Packing the bag or basket
Equipment needed

a flat-bottomed bag or basket
2 paper serviettes
a few paper handkerchiefs
a polythene container or bag
   or tinfoil to pack sausage rolls

2 plastic cups or thermos cups
   for the soup
2 plastic or paper plates
2 plastic knives and forks
2 teaspoons for the mousse

1 Put all the items on the table so that nothing is forgotten.

2 The bag you choose to put the food in should have a flat base so that the things can be packed firm and not roll around.

3 Put the food and thermos in first. Then wrap the knives, forks and spoons in the paper handkerchiefs or serviettes. To prevent things from rattling, fit the plates and other items you want to take in the gaps around the food.

4 When you have eaten, either find a bin to leave the rubbish or else bring it home.

Festival Cakes

The Festivals we celebrate in this country are religious ones, Christmas Day and Easter Sunday. The foods which we connect with these Festivals have no religious meaning, but are more national dishes, for example, Christmas cakes, mincepies, turkey and plum pudding at Christmastime, and Easter eggs and Hot-cross buns at Easter.

Decorating cakes is fun but you must allow yourself plenty of time. It is not something to do in a hurry otherwise you will make a mess of it. Decorated cakes tend to be rich so only serve small portions at a time. All cakes, large or small, should be kept fresh in an air-tight container, for example, a biscuit tin or a polythene box.

Chocolate Log

Food to collect

1 Swiss roll filled with jam
6 equal portions of soft butter
  (see page 9)
6 heaped tablespoons of icing
  sugar

Equipment to collect

a piece of cardboard 2 in/5 cm
  longer and wider than the
  Swiss roll
scissors, pencil, tinfoil, ruler
a mixing bowl

6 equal portions
butter 6oz 170g

6 heaped tbsps.
icing sugar 6oz 170g

A medium size bar
plain chocolate 4oz 115g

a medium-sized bar of plain
    chocolate
2 drops of vanilla essence

a wooden spoon
greaseproof paper
a sieve
1 tablespoon and teaspoon
a palette knife
a fork
2 basins
a saucer to stand the bottle of
    vanilla essence on

Decorations
a robin
holly leaves

a saucepan
a kettle

Preparation

* Wash your hands. Put on your apron.
* Collect the food and equipment. Put on the work-top.
* First make a cardboard base, covered with tinfoil for the log.

Making the cardboard base

1 Measure the length and width of the Swiss roll with a ruler.
Then add 2 in/5 cm to both the length and the width.
2 Measure this out on the cardboard. Mark it with a pencil and
join up the lines. You should have an oblong shape.
Cut along the lines with a pair of paper scissors.
3 Place the cut-out cardboard on a piece of tinfoil. The tinfoil
needs to be 1 in/2·5 cm bigger than the cardboard all the way
round, so it can be folded underneath. Mark the tinfoil, join
up the lines, then cut out.
4 Place the cardboard in the middle of the tinfoil. First fold over
the two short ends. Then fold along the two long sides. Turn
the cardboard over and you should have a nice smooth base.

Method for decoration: making chocolate buttercream

1 Boil some water in a kettle.
2 Break the bar of chocolate into a basin.